The Sound of the Collective Pen

A Poetry Anthology by Emerging Voices

Curated by

BookButler Publishing Company

The Sound of the Collective Pen:
A Poetry Anthology by Emerging Voices

Published by BookButler Publishing Company

Upper Marlboro, MD 20774

TheBookButler.com

ISBN: 9781967082681 (Paperback)
ISBN: 9781967082698 (eBook)
Library of Congress Control Number: 2025921982
Cover & Interior Design by Aaron C. Butler
Printed in the United States of America

BookButler Publishing Company titles may be purchased in bulk for educational, business, fundraising, or sales promotional use. For information, please email: info@thebookbutler.com

Dedication

For the poets who wrote with courage,
and the readers who receive their voices
with an open heart.

Table of contents

Introduction

A poem begins with a spark — a thought, a memory, a heartbeat that insists on being heard. It flows from the hand, ink tracing the quiet truths we carry, the loud questions we dare to ask, the beauty we sometimes forget to see.

The Sound of the Collective Pen gathers sparks from poets across the nation (and the UK), each one a voice with its own rhythm, its own shade of light and shadow. Together, they form a constellation of words — stories and dreams stitched into a single book

Here you will find verses that whisper comfort, cries that resist, echoes that heal, and ballads of love. You will hear rhythms that imagine tomorrow, and a final chorus bold and unafraid. Some poems will remain with you like a soft echo; others will strike with the certainty of a drumbeat.

This anthology is not just a collection of poems — it is a meeting place. A gathering of pens that, when set to the page, become a single, resounding voice. May you read slowly, linger in the pauses, and let the sound of these voices find a home in your heart.

The Sound of the Collective Pen

Opening Poem

It is not one voice—
but many.
Not one story—
but a chorus of truths.

Ink spills,
and silence breaks.
Lines rise like marching feet,
like rivers refusing to be dammed.

Every stroke
is a heartbeat.
Every word
a declaration.

Together,
these voices become thunder—
rolling across the page,
leaving no corner of the soul untouched.

This is more than poetry.
This is the sound of the collective pen.

— Aaron C. Butler

Chapter 1:
Whispers of Origin

Identity, heritage, family, ancestry, self-image.

The first sound is not silence, but a whisper — of names remembered, of places that shaped us, of stories whispered through time. These poems hum with ancestry and beginnings, reminding us that who we are resonates in both reflection and inheritance, holding family, memory, and legacy in their breath.

Breath of Origin

Before the ink,
before the word,
before the shaping of names,
there was breath.

A whisper rising in the chest,
a hush that trembled into sound,
a thread connecting silence to life.

Every story begins here—
not in nation or tongue,
not in color or creed,
but in the simple rhythm
of inhale and exhale,
the music of being.

We are born into air shared,
into lungs that swell alike,
into the first sound we make—
a cry, a gasp,
a proof of existence.

And though the world
will later divide,
build walls and borders,
the breath remembers—
it is one,
it is many,
it is origin.

— Genesis Lyric

The First Gift: Inheritance

Before names,
before stories were divided,
we were given the same inheritance:
sky,
river,
soil,
light.

The sun did not choose sides.
The rain did not fall for one people alone.
The stars carved their maps
for every traveler who looked up.

Even now,
the ground beneath our feet
is a common ancestor—
holding the weight of all who walk it,
keeping record in stone and root.

We inherit the turning of seasons,
the chorus of morning birds,
the hush of falling snow.

This earth is the first legacy,
a gift we did not earn
yet carry forward—
together,
as one.

— Noah Rivers

In My Skin

Shades of beauty GOD made them all.
Medium, light, and sometimes dark.
What if I looked like Him,
so light, so bright?

Not loving the tint
the Heavenly FATHER for us was meant.
Beautiful is your tone;
never feel ugly in the one you own.

Embrace yourself whether dark, medium, or light;
all are beautiful in God's sight.
A childhood bruise
somehow made your confidence lose.

Forget not WHO put in place
all colors of the human race.
Laid down self-love;
embrace that skin given from above.

Don't hurt others aiming for a higher place
because inside yourself, you have come to hate.
First, you give me a hug,
then my complexion you're ready to judge.

Some say light skin has its way;
I wish I was light for just one day.
Others say she's light
and think she's cute, so full of pride.

Maybe she's crying and hiding
the pain deep inside.
Got the job, the position, it's her tone.
She has no smarts—
just her shade got her the part.

YES, she has a brain.
From uncaring words,
what do you wish to gain?
Blaming others, reflecting day after day,
reminds you of the things you years ago
heard someone say.

Still, remember WHO put that color on your face.
See beauty, not disgust.
Open your eyes; look, you must.
Every day hug yourself and say,
GOD surely did not make a mistake.

Variety of shades makes us all,
like Winter, Spring, Summer, and Fall.

Some say give me a hand;
I only want just a little tan.
End self-dislike of your skin—
that neither you nor I could put us in.

Charmed by the world's standard of beauty,
seems we're confused. Where is our true duty?

Don't be at odds nor in despair;
we all have a cross to bear.
A tone for all, even me—
we're GOD'S own masterpiece.

Love the skin
that we didn't put ourselves in.

What if the zebra to the tiger says,
"Let's trade stripes for a portion of the day?"
Tiger says to Zebra, "I don't like your stripes or your fur,
not even a cat or its purr."

Suppose a rose could somehow think:
"I don't really like the color that I own."
Says hey flower lily, "I want your tone,
that pretty one that is on your petal."

Seems always a tone battle.
Stop and smell the beautiful flowers—
that color and fur that is meant to be ours.

See GOD's formation, HIS origination.
High self-esteem needed in a changing generation.
Embrace happily the skin designed for each to love,
which is given from The One above.

— Annie C. Maclin-Johnson

Black Is Me

Black is me, shown in the color of my skin
and texture of my hair—
the race I totally own.

God formed me in this darkness;
I definitely embrace my Blackness.

This Blackness is not to be tried
because I'm not that kind of guy, so don't try.
Black is me—
I always try to be kind,
so don't try messing with my mind;
I don't want to get a fine.

Black is me.
I see so many smiles when I speak
that it inspires me to strive each day
to reach my highest peak.

My heritage is beautiful,
and I will forever be proud of my Blackness.
I can't be swayed by foolishness,
won't let obstacles stop me.
I just want to be a conqueror and be free.

Black is me!

Adversity comes on every hand,
but I fight on because Black is me.
My confidence allows me to achieve all my goals
and to help save so many lost souls.

Black is me,
and I can be what I want to be.
As you can see—
Black is me.

— Cassandra Reed-Anderson

Me

How can I be anyone other than me?
All I know is myself.
My personality is original—
that's all I can be.
Why should I change?
What should the change be?

My gifts, my energy, my stature and handsomeness—
this is just me.

How can I be anyone other than me?
At every turn they envy,
even those who heard sometimes
hate what they can't see.

I'm me, naturally grown over time,
matured like the finest tree.

Do their eyes betray them—can they see?
I don't wear a mask.
My true self is all I can be.

When I'm an asset, I'm loved and wanted.
But when I'm down,
love turns to deceit.
How can this be?

The trials of life have come against me.

My own heart—
a weapon used against me it would be.
Heart heavy, I might lose a pound
as sorrow hollows me.

I will overcome, succeed,
and manifest greatness
despite if things look bleak.

— Ky'Lee Jamal

What About My Nose and Mouth?

What about my nose and mouth—
for laughs and grins, you soon blurt out:
"Look at that big nose and mouth."

This time, giggles you have gained,
caring not, I drown in pain.

You search, you scan,
poking fun as you glance.
My nose and mouth are not like yours—
small, petite, so cute, and adored.

Amusing yourself at my suffering cost,
wish I could run and ignore your mocks.
You may not understand my place—
did someone in times past
make jokes about you and laugh?

Why do you voice such careless words?
I wish they sound more like hummingbirds.
Instead of songs that birds sing,
I see chilling eyes like bees that stings.

Joking as you walk by, then pause,
giggling so hard, you stumble and fall,
gazing through your tear-soaked eyeballs.

GOD made all features,
living things and creatures.

Your gloomy words, like rain and clouds,
hanging over my head you seem so proud.
Feeling sad within and without,
stop right now; I want to shout
as I listen to those words: "big nose, and mouth."

Chuckling loudly behind my back,
kind hearts are what so many lack.
Standing around with your friends,
insulting me to no end.

Have you any shame?
Your snubs are like burning flames.
Show someone today that you care—
some kind words you wish to share?

Heard someone say you took a trip
to get injections in your lips.
It may be me who's wounded now;
could it be you next time somehow?

In this mixed-up human race,
today I plan to own my space
with this nose and mouth
that's on my face.

—Annie C. Maclin-Johnson

Thank God for Picking My Mother

I thank you God
for picking my Mother
a time I can't get back
a time I will always have

I thank you God
for picking my Mother
the memories will remind me
of the love
she so carefully wove and nurtured

I thank you God
for picking my Mother
to send me off with just enough tweaking
on this racist and ever trying journey
self-assured and confident as I
stand on your rock, Lord
knowing that through her ever-capable hands
I am enough -

I thank you God
for picking my Mother
may her legacy of love
embolden my steps
in the grand
Sea of Humanity…

— Sierra Leone Dixon

Parents

My parents were two wonderful people,
with two different personalities
and two unique ways of showing love.

I loved them both, and I know they loved me.
I know they loved each other.
We enjoyed life together.

They were always my
"Mommy" and "Daddy."
I didn't know how short a time I would have with them.

I'm glad they were my friends,
as well as my parents.
I'm glad they taught me how to treat myself,
as well as others.

Road trips, partying, gambling, and loving.
I've been alive longer now
than the years I had them.
I know they loved me.

My mother was accidentally given an overdose
of medication in the hospital and died.

My father couldn't believe the news;
cried and bled out, three weeks later.
The doctors said it was a broken heart.
Depression.
I know it was love.

Because of my parents, I came to be.
I learned how to treat people,
enjoy and love life,
and believe in GOD.

— Graemme Denyce Boone

Hannah Faye's Faith

Hannah was my Amazing Grace.
Hannah, my mom, conceived and birthed me
in good Faith.

Hannah's heart was gold,
like her mother Magnolia.
She had so much wisdom.
Hannah lived to be 75.

Hannah was boss in charge.
Her love was sweet and giving,
no holds barred.

Hannah, I'm forever grateful because as
my mother, Hannah's love was and always will be unshakeable.

Hannah was powerful,
bad in a good way.
I miss Hannah's unshakeable love
every single day.

Hannah Faye's faith was so, so strong.
I know my mother, Hannah, will never
leave me alone.

They say people are there to catch when you fall…
without Hannah Faye Pitts-Galmore Davis
I would not be here at all.

— IZR Galmore

MK Forever

My mother moved me out of Southeast for a reason.
She didn't want it to become hunting season
for me and my brothers.

It was seven of us—
we didn't even know what was going to hit us
on this earth as our lives dispersed.

I had to pick up the pieces
we didn't even know we lost.
But as we lost,
we tried to pick up the cost—
but we didn't know who was the boss.
So therefore, we lost.

For God to give us a win,
He said, If you follow these rules
you will go ahead and ascend.

If you lost the power of your pen,
maybe you could win.

So I ask of you to honor the lives
of Michael Edward Morgan
and Kareem Ilighsa Palmer—

because death don't separate us,
our love don't separate us.

We had to learn
what the ancestors meant to us,
because they were taken from us
when we crossed the sea.

But as we saw the sea,
we started to believe—
and we received wisdom:
their lives mattered.

— Shantie Morgan

Magnolia

Magnolia was a light,
a smile so beautiful and bright.
Magnolia's love now sits,
and comes from Heaven above.

Magnolia lived to be 94.
She shall be loved forevermore,
even though she died in 2019.
Magnolia Penny Pitts was truly
a Queen.

Magnolia's love,
Magnolia's taste,
forever I will miss
Magnolia's grace.

Grace she had,
grace she is.
Magnolia made Newberry a great
place to live.

Magnolia's heart was also gold.
She never left me or others
out in the cold.

Magnolia I miss in my heart, you see.
Magnolia was a great part
of our family tree.

Grandmother Magnolia Penny Pitts,
you are forever in our hearts.

Dedicated to My Grandmother, Mrs. Magnolia P. Pitts (b. 1923 –
d. 2019)

We Miss You...
Willie Davis (son-in-law)
James C. Galmore (grandson)
Mason W. Gibbs, Boyd C. Barnett III, Jamon J. Galmore (3 great grandsons)

— IZR Galmore

My PG County in the 90s

Jumpin' out the Arbor View apartment window,
shortcuttin' our way to the 7-11 'cross the street.
We hung out all summer eve
on Brinkley Road,
at the entryway of building 201.
Sitting on the rotted farm fence,
showing off our ghetto tudes,
smells of apartment hallways –
I smile at the pungent whiff of nostalgia –
remembering the brief moments of freedom
before pitch blackness.
The streetlights must not been working those nights,
or maybe the moon held off on our behalf.
Peeing in the bush
cause the lil white boy said I could.
Maybe his daddy ain't teach him the old adage,
"What goes on in the house stays in the house."
Or maybe he wasn't raised
on beatings and secrecy.
Either way,
I got my ass whooped that day.

We lived off spaghetti
and roasted chicken during the week
and the weekend eats came free
from family's part-time jobs
at Pigs in a Blanket,
Popeyes,
Little Caesar's,
and Black Eye Peas.
Rivertown employed us as we explored
the family five-finger discounts,
sticky theater floors and seats,
Kmart clothes shopping

as we sipped on cherry slushies,
boring linen store perusing,
bank deposits and withdrawals,
glass-bottled Pepsi and a pack of Newports,
"take this ten dollars and fill up on 7."
Black folk, my folk, us folk,
we always stuck together.

So many memories of my PG in the 90s.

Gotta run down Eastover right quick
get some braidin' hair and blue magic
for the Friday fry days.
Smells of burnt hair filled the air,
kitchen necks and sizzled cartilage from my ear
"you betta keep still for I slap the black off ya."
Momma was lethal with that hot comb
I was cussin' her ass out in my head tho.

Saturday's morning bacon permeated our home.
Eggs cooked in bacon grease
with flimsy slices of KRAFT cheese
we were always broke, but never poor.
Dad gets the first waffle – tradition was king.
Two to three waffles each for bro and me
I always tried to keep up.

Sunday dresses, shiny shoes,
dolled up for Sunrise service blues.
Sunday afternoons Dad's mac & cheese,
overcooked green beans,
taters and dinner rolls,
smells of fried chicken grease embedded in our clothes.

Beggin' to go outside every day
playin' hide'n go seek and relay race,
baseball with a tennis ball and a pole
from the clothesline,
back flips off the neighbor's hill,
handlebars and no seat havin' bike rides,
racing after ice cream trucks,
Fort Foote Market five-cent candy fill-ups,
climbing trees and negro knockin',
"don't be comin' in and out this house
lettin' all my air condition out,"
water hose drinkin'
Mary Mack singin'
street car dodgin'
double dutch jumpin'
hopscotch skippin'
dirt pie makin'
caterpillar holdin'
firefly catchin'
and we never missed a beat.

What y'all know 'bout my PG in the 90s?

— Sharese Simone

Daffodils

Almost 30 years in the writing business—
think of me as daffodils.

I grow from strength to strength until I've died.
I'm like Coca-Cola, I'm vintage but I still have my fizz.

Established in 1996, still I'm giving you my lyrical drink.
In 2014, I was awarded a certificate by United Press
for dedication poet.

2025, I'm still thriving.

Albert Johnson, aka Prodigy from Mobb Deep,
quoted the letter I had written to him—
it had a lot of intelligence in it.

I don't want to blow my own trumpet,
but you've got to hear it.

When I die, I just don't want people to tread.
I want people to remember me
by thinking of the words I thought at the top of my head.

Not all of my poems are decent—
sometimes they could make you bend.

I feel like from that seed that was sown,
a legend was born.

My petals get wet,
but my stalks won't be torn.

In the soil, I make those dents
and grace your lawns.

I thank the heavens above
for the light that shines.

To whoever gave me this blessing,
I haven't conquered my achievements.

I always write straight from the heart.
I can't give up, I'm too strong.

Somebody once told me I was blessed.
I know I give a round of applause
to my mind and right hand—
they deserve more.

I can't afford to lose my balance and fall off.
I'm going to avoid those accidents and stay on.

Poetry has and will always be in my blood.
I just need to make it grow up.

I don't ride anybody else's bikes—
they can never take me off.

I ride mine,
it's where I belong.

— Natalie B. Peterson

Linwood Edward

I miss you like a fat kid loves cake.
I try to keep your name on my tongue for God's sake.
No one on this earth knew me like you.
Aw man, we made it do what it do.

I forever love you.
I was always your squirrel,
Daddy's precious baby girl.

You gave me light, humor, confidence, and dance—
this world couldn't even stand a chance.

As I glance on our lives together,
how amazing it feels.
Got to go on the drills,
always gonna have good laughs and with a lil feels.

That's my dad, I love him so much.
My mind, my heart, my spirit
will never let you go.

As I continue to grow, I have your face—
no one could never get it…
this place
forsake
for those that did not know.

When they see your daughter,
I will daggone put on a show.

Forever yours, my Virgo man.
Even though you was little—
ahh, you stood grand.

Papi, I love you forever and forever.
You will always be with me.

I love you.

Your dearest daughter,
Shantie.

— Shantie Morgan

Four Eyes Advantage

Four eyes are better than two.
Children need four eyes—
two just won't do.

Each child with diverse needs,
building self-worth is planting the seed.
Strong minds and stability help them succeed.

A set of two is what was meant;
half of four was never the intent.
Can't grow. Some moms and dads cannot see;
two eyes won't nourish into a healthy grown tree—
only a stump and half of what a child could be.

Dad by himself, Mom on her own,
two eyes are missing from the home.
A portion of a tree will never bear fruit;
four eyes are needed, not just a deuce.
Two eyes miss what is needed from four,
especially when evil comes knocking at their door.

Those who love you know what evil deeds have done;
you won't regret their advice in the long run.
Not your fault, no… not at all;
with four eyes watching, they may not fall.
High expectations… so many letdowns,
crying out… I need you… Mom!… Dad!… please come around.

Alone… Dad might miss this or that,
but Mom is there and she has his back.
Two plus two eyes which equals four;
when they cry and their tears pour.

Raising them alone… trying to be two
seems impossible with all that only one has to do.
Family design needs four eyes… but many have only two.

A child tumbles… almost crumbles;
four eyes say, Get up; I'll help you through your stumbles.
Look… the child's life is falling apart,
pretending to be happy… while hiding a broken heart.

Relationships ruined… feelings down through and through;
all humans need guidance… one who's the family glue.

— Annie C. Maclin-Johnson

Dear Daughter,

Don't let hopelessness beat ya
Don't let life defeat ya
Don't be afraid to try
Don't be afraid to cry
But do be afraid
not to live

As seasons must change
Things can't always be the same
Sometimes hellos become good-byes
But don't forget the twinkle
Of the stars in the skies

Don't always know when to let go
Can't always tell the fast from the slow
But love yourself - no matter what goes down
Always be left with your feet on the ground

As new doors open, old doors close
Do you suppose
It's just how life was meant to be
Don't be afraid to live
Don't be afraid to give
The only guarantee that will always
see you through
Is YOU...

— Sierra Leone Dixon

Odesscia's...Song

My sister, Odesscia,
was very beautiful.
She loved to sing.
She eventually married happily and got a ring.

Her voice was soulful,
and she sang so true.
I know angels in Heaven,
on that heavenly choir,
loved welcoming you.

My sister was bad like no other;
that's why I'm glad she was my older sister—
since we already had… a brother.

We miss you now,
we miss you dearly.
Every lyric you sang
kept you near me.

Near my heart,
in my ear,
I can hear you still singing,
my dear.

My dearest sister Odesscia,
sister whom I love,
is on that celestial choir jamming
in Heaven above.

Above the stars,
I hope you are—
singing and dancing,
because you are a star.

Sister Odesscia, you are singing so good.
You encouraged me to do the best I could.
The best I can, I'll strive to be—
Odesscia "Desa" Galmore-Barnett.

— IZR Galmore

B.I.W.I.A

Brown is what I am.
No man, woman or child is going to change this colour of tan.

Some people don't believe in that.
Me bleach my skin?
Are you mad?
This is the complexion i 'am supposed to have.

If only i could make them understand.
Every skin-lightening cream should be banned.
It's getting into the wrong hands.

Whoever is manufacturing it, must be really angry at Africa, man.
They must have some serious contempt for the African man.

What is this telling the upcoming generation on the land?
That it's alright to hype these so-called brands?

Do these consumers know what these product are designated for?
It's there to balance serious dark marks with your skin.
What's the purpose—in keep using it more and more?

Just remember, once the melanin is damaged,
you can never start from the beginning.
Your complexion is now white to the core.

Why do you hate the skin that you are in?
You can't make the Caucasians win.

It's also destroying for the kids who's mixed-race.
They might think they're a sin,
to start destroying their own skin.

Back in the day black parents had to go left,
and the white parents had to go right.
The mixed business often went anywhere like rubbish.

These products make us hate ourselves.
Still, we're purchasing it from the shelves.
The retailers are definitely on something else.
They love too much wealth—
even if it melts the living daylights out of us,
the african skin health.

Would you take this unlawful beauty she is,
because B.I.W.I.A.

— Natalie B. Peterson

Ode to Grandma Nissi

"Speak a word of gratitude and dignity
at the mention of Grandma Nissi's name.

Celebrate the strength and courage she showed
in every situation, always the same."

If you were caught in the wrong,
you knew Grandma Nissi's wrath was coming for you!
She would first give you strong correction with her lips,
a stern look and hands on her hips.

Then she'd break out humming a specific note
to calm things down a bit—
whispering how you had lost your mind,
made a shameful slip!

And when it was time to leave out,
we left with favor, hope, blessings for our tomorrows,
equipped with wisdom's grand treasures
and our perseverance put to the ultimate test.

The inevitable would abide alongside,
threatening our determination to thrive.
Yet our core strong, fixed on the balance
of life's mountain joys and valley sorrows.

"Thank You, Grandma Nissi
Guardian of faith you were indeed.
Thank You for the many love-n-life lessons you taught us,
for embracing and sheltering me."

— Mildred M. Stokes

Breaking Generational Curses

Sh'Quelle:
I was told love was

Ari:
silent.
Hidden in chaos.

Sh'Quelle:
Carried like a secret,
wrapped in shame.

Ari:
But secrets don't grow flowers,
they grow weeds.

Sh'Quelle:
And I refuse to hand you weeds.
I refuse to pass down roots
that choke instead of nourish.

Ari:
I was born for gardens,
for light,
for hands that knew gentleness first.

Sh'Quelle:
I learned too early that survival

Ari:
was mistaken for love.

Sh'Quelle:
And silence

Ari:
was mistaken for strength.

Together:
But we are not repeating
that story.

Sh'Quelle:
When rage knocked at my door,
I swallowed it whole.

Ari:
But you taught me
that swallowing fire
only burns from the inside.

Sh'Quelle:
So I taught you,
"If you feel the flame

Ari:
let it roar and if you have to burn it
let it burn to the ground."

Sh'Quelle:
Because your anger

Ari:
is not danger.

Together:
It is boundary.

Ari:
And when I asked,
"What is family?"

Sh'Quelle:
I did not say blood,
or duty,
or blind loyalty.

Ari:
You said

Together:
"Family is the love that doesn't make you
feel like you are choosing them over yourself."

Sh'Quelle:
I was given wounds

Ari:
but I was given healing.

Sh'Quelle:
I was handed silence

Ari:
but I was handed voice.

Sh'Quelle:
I was taught to endure

Ari:
but I was taught to rise.

Together:
We are the breaking,
we are the bridge,
we are the beginning.

Sh'Quelle:
The chain ends

Ari:
with us.

Together:
A new cycle begins here.

Sh'Quelle:
They say parents are the teachers

Ari:
but I have been teaching you too.

Sh'Quelle:
I thought I would show you the world

Ari:
but I was the one holding your hand
when you saw purpose in it again.

Sh'Quelle:
You remind me to stop

Ari:
to look at the butterfly,
the dandelion,
the sky that looks too big for one person to hold.

Sh'Quelle:
You remind me that joy
isn't hidden in grand things

Ari:
it's tucked inside the ordinary.

Sh'Quelle:
When the world told me to harden,
you softened me.

Ari:
When the years tried to steal your laughter,
I returned it.

Sh'Quelle:
When the past weighed heavy

Ari:
I became the reason you set it down.
And Mama, you taught me

Sh'Quelle:
no, baby.
You taught me.

Ari:
No, we teach each other.

Together:
That love is not one-sided.
It is a circle,
always returning,
always beginning again.

Sh'Quelle:
You are proof that life

Ari:
is still beautiful.

Sh'Quelle:
You are proof that broken things

Ari:
can still grow flowers.

Together:
You are proof
that I was meant to be,
here.

—Sh'Quelle Brown & Aryianna Edmond

Chapter 2:
Cries of Resistance

Struggle, survival, injustice, trauma, protest, truth-telling.

When the world throws stones, the pen pushes back. When silence breaks, it does not break gently. These poems rise as cries — sharp, raw, unrelenting — pounding like drums against injustice. Struggle becomes fire, and fire becomes language, forcing the world to listen.

The Mirror They Threw

My world shattered—
splintered into a million
jagged fragments
of my mind.

the glass embedded
into my skin,
and I begged forgiveness
for sins that weren't mine.

crimson pain
flooded my heart,
an orchestra of lies
and deceit,
playing a requiem
no child should hear.

they said
I broke the mirror,
but no one asked
who threw it.

no one saw
the rage behind their eyes,
the storm behind the silence,
the way shame
was passed down
like an heirloom.

I gathered the shards
like holy things—
delicate, dangerous,
glinting with memory.
I pressed them

into poems
because no one else
was listening.

I bled meaning
onto every page,
stitched metaphors
where open wounds once wept.

and then the time came—
a moment quiet
as breath before flight—
and from those shards
rose a thousand butterflies,
their wings trembling
with the weight
of what I survived.

suspended in air
for just a second,
in that stillness,
I saw myself—
not broken,
but becoming.
not ruined,
but remade.
a girl forged
in glass and grief,
now soaring
in spite of it all.

— Amy Michelle Kennedy

Boy Blue

There was a boy who watched the world
through prison bars as others hurled,
the taunts and jeers like children do
that mocked this sparrow's gallows view.

To fly away the boy would dream
unfurling wings on jets of stream,
that soared above the piercing blows
then feather slept where kindness grows.

But in his cage this boy withstood
a thistle perch that often would,
dismount him onto fecal ground
that festered with each tearful sound.

Until the boy outgrew the cage
but not the depths of dormant rage,
gestating without conscience care
aborting any hope or prayer.

That one day all the taunts and jeers
would vaporize and disappear,
from crypts inside this sparrow's mind
instead of hate in full rewind.

To which this story has to go
where aftermaths will always show,
that innocence reduced to swine
comes home to roost in Columbine.

— Andrew Kouroupos

Diary of a Broken Dream

I have nothing—
that's what they always told me.
But they don't understand why we sell with the homies,
or why we ball so hard to receive plastic trophies.

And every shot's a fade,
and a scream that says Kobe,
because every shot's a fade,
and a bullet struck too deep—

for survival.

We've been cursed since arrival.
The government is our rival.
We have no guidance,
so we worship hip hop idols.

The police don't protect us;
they were taught to neglect us.
Like the politicians that create laws to subject us,
but never really find our needs
or properly represent us.

Because we were considered property since the first president,
and we weren't guaranteed life since the first precedent.
So selling rocks to buy ice doesn't mean an ill intent;
it's a way to get by when the struggle circumvents,
or a way to get back time that we feel that we've spent.

Because if we freeze our minds,
nothing really exists.

No matter how vivid you paint the picture,
some people have no vision
and can't see the consequences of their decisions.
They're actors,
they're acting.

They say "packing never lacking"
but the cycle is everlasting.

They run themselves ragged
in drug traffic.
And if you aren't talking right,
they pull the automatic.

You hear sirens blare and radio static.
Suicide and murder is the new dynamic.
Children go and play,
but they always have their bikes,
because every day they know
they'll be running home from fights.

They'll be beaten black and blue,
they'll be crying to their mothers,
not knowing what to do,
not understanding how they're governed.

Lost in a system that wasn't made for them.
Lost in a system that has no space for them.
Laws within the system try to cage them in.

In the land of the free
and the home of the brave—

but the bravest ones
are those who hung on the stage
and hung on the gallows.

We're taught to bow our heads
as the truth unravels.
Instead we duck and dodge,
and get hammered by the gavel.

The streets isn't the only place that we're beat.
In classrooms, Black kids feel like they can't compete.
And when they flash news,
it's not complete without a homicide.

There's no more Jack and Jill—
we just run and hide.
There's no more playground games,
because it's battle time.

Melanin like elbow grease—
they call it grit and grime.

Because every day is a fight for the next one.
So they just sit outside and hope that the check comes.
They don't want to starve,
because that's how death comes.

But when another soldier dies,
we call them the blessed one,
because they no longer live a life that oppressed them.

A life where we are killed
because we wanted new sneakers.
A life where we are killed
because we blast our speakers.
A life where we are killed
even though we work 'til our knees hurt.

In the end I'm thankful,
'cause I know it could be worse.
But it's hard to have faith
when there's always a new pyre,
another body killed by gunfire.

It's hard to have our heart's desires
when society labels us as thieves and liars.
But we are more than our street attire.

We are young kings and queens—
something higher.

— Kaamilah Diabaté

Ice Iced Baby

Ice Iced baby—coldest administration of the 21st century.
Because of Order Made, I am now a part of America's history.

No mention of his name, because mentioning the name of evil
will only give it power.
Turned the world upside down within 24 hours.

News of the order spread across social media.
People screaming, kids crying—
this just became a mass hysteria.

Immediate concern of my lover's safety,
wondering if he would be affected.
What rights did he hold,
was his freedom protected?

Received a couple of concerning calls,
asking if everything was ok.
As usual, my lover replied positively—
that all was fine and not to worry.

A few days passed,
and he kissed me goodbye as he was heading out the door.
My intuition felt something was off
but no reason as to why.

My dear lover circled back, kissed me,
and said he loved me one more time.
Once he left out the door,

the ICE enforcement met him outside.

The doorbell rang and caused my heart
to fall into my chest.
Could not understand why officers were standing
outside of my address.

Opened the door and was handed all his belongings.
Asked what was going on,
but was left with strange silence
and thoughts of wondering.

Headed to the living room and collapsed,
struggling to breathe.
Shouted out to God,
"Why are you doing this to me?"

God did not answer.
There was no response—
left alone to feel the pain
and wipe the tears from crying.

The many days and nights of wavering cries,
mixed with sobbing, aching that intensified.
Having to face with the conscious fact
that the nights of slumber would be alone.

Days were battles to awake,
do something useful to make it count,
always hoping the: what, when, and how
became known.

No Independence celebration in the area,
many people hiding in their homes,
too afraid to be a part of civilization—

too many loved ones detained and gone.

Making calls, sending emails,
mailing letters to officials falling on deaf ears.
No updates, no information.
A mother's facial heartbreak,
words of pain but never tears.

Ice Iced baby—coldest administration of my time.
Left alone to feel ICE's frozen touch,
and to deal with the tapestry of horrified thoughts
that linger daily in my mind.

Five long months have passed.
Pleading to God for a sign,
that our loved one will return home
and everything will turn out fine.

— T. Smith

Woman Behind The Smoke (screwballs)

Too much 'screwballs' vacate this world.
Frankly I am fed-up with it.
Too much femicide be taking over the world,
but nobody's doing a thing about it.

Those 'screwballs' aren't even man-made.
It's what's been created by you, deep within your brains.
The chemical imbalance is making the blood boil in my veins,
to the point where my perception is going to come across as pure
rage.

I'm just expressing from my side of my lane.
Hands-up, who's going to confess that they're also a screwball,
other than me?
A positive and constructive one.
I do not drive nobody up the wall—
only those sick-in-the-heads type of screwballs drive me up the
wall.

Do I have a something against the mentally unstable?
How can I?
A part of me do not like it when they prey on the vulnerable.
I too lost my mind.
Overall, I have never made society uncomfortable.

Screwballs continue to threaten my personal safety.
Those screwballs do not deserve none.
For a long time now, i have always been paranoid of any type of
screwball—
both men and women.
I've already been there.

I watch how fellow screwballs be lunging at me with their claws,
violating my atmosphere.

If I was on this type of thing,
just watch how fast the police will be on my case.
I'm the victim here, not doing any anything.

Yet when it comes to the chasing, who's doing the running?
The woman who just wants to be free of harassment.
I want these screwballs to keep their distance.
This is going to be nonexistent
until the government helps the reins of the innocent.

Let's say a schizophrenic woman pulled the trigger on a genuine
screwball.
Why doesn't the government stop this sexism nonsense with us
women,
and start listening out for our concerns and fears as well?

Screwballs should not be allowed to harass any woman
for whatever the reason.
Too many women have already been violated.
It just adds to the advances.
No woman should ever have to experience this.

All the stuff you screwballs are on—
from a female perspective it is wrong.
Where do the screwballs get off displaying the wrong?
Making them feel so macho and superior
that us women won't stand up to them.

We are the female species that's sacrificing our wombs for (men)
like you.
And that's how you screwballs repay (us) back.
That could never be felt in a million years.

You screwballs think the universe revolves around you.
You make me see more than clear.
Like I was not analyzing society already—
got me questioning my sanity.

Is something mentally wrong with me?
Is my paranoia ringing too many alarms?
Professionals, I have a burning question—
and somebody better answer.

When I inform you somebody is mentally unstable,
do not dash my accusations out of the window.
It's not a question if, they're mental.
They're mental.

Twenty years of being stable—
I did not maintain my sanity for nothing.
I can often recognize when professionals just be turning a blind
eye.
They could've been snorting coke.

No, not the fizzy cans of pop,
but the street drugs making their brains go pop.
Forever intoxicated, now they can't cope,
having no peers to smoke with.
Now they're walking the streets alone,
displaying the traits of a messed-up screwball.

Every day there is no potential.
Every day there is no motivation.
Can't find the tendency just to be a bit normal,
by turning into psychotic fools
with no thought of whoever they choose to harass.

As long as you screwballs be getting your kicks,
it should be them getting the kicks
for their sick and twisted fuels.

Their should be making they parents proud,
bettering and making something out of themselves.
Don't give me nothing about how the system failed you.
You failed within the system.

They're too twisted to be putting their heads into books,
instead of dwelling on the wrath with what pushed you out.
You screwballs need to be checking yourselves out.

Do not take me, nor any other woman for any bait.
It is you screwballs who needs the help.
I'm no longer under the authority of the men in white coats.
Been there, had that.

It's your time screwballs to be restrained and injected
by the men in white coats.
What, me have pity?
This is my worst nightmare.

Throw that messed-up sanity elsewhere.
Take a long walk screwballs on a short bridge.
The same way you make me feel inferior,
putting me on edge.

The constant routine of looking over my shoulder—
this paranoia getting me all vexed and stressed.
How would you screwballs like it if the tables were turned back
onto you?

Your sanity has nothing but bad intentions.
Didn't your fathers not show you the ropes
of how to respect and have compassion for women's well-being?

Then again their sanity has been deteriorated like broken chairs.
Could it be fixed?
Even if they did get the opportunity, they might oppose it.

Think, when a mentally unstable person is unwell,
the greater risk of femicide be is actually rising.
Screwballs think I do not know what they're up to—
following me on the side,
just to mentally harass me.

Get some therapy.
They visualize the world like their land,
where every person is messed up.
This is not how you were when you came from your mums.

I'm not going to sit back,
watching these screwballs pass and last,
launching mental and physical attacks.

Prescribed medication disposed of on our pavements,
when it does have an oral use.
Right now, I want to put you screwball necks into nooses
and pull the cord.

— Natalie B. Peterson

Rebel Son

Awakened at the crest of dawn
to rubble under risen sun,
my hunger beckons both my eyes
to feast on what their hate has done.

I slept despite starvation's waft
beguiling me with every breath,
that I in all my innocence
will not be faced with martyr's death.

Yet I am still a sapling tree
an unripe fig on Gaza Street,
a sweetness that was once to be
is now a bitter fruit to eat.

To this I rise a rebel son
who cannot dream that he will dine,
with Jacob's line when all he sees
is genocide in Palestine.

— Andrew Kouroupos

Pronouns

What do I call you again?
Swear this isn't on purpose.
My naïve mind is trying to understand—
She/Her, He/Him,
which is correct with the They/Their or Them?

So confused as to how to address who,
trying to avoid the misgendering,
but still unaware of whom is who.

Ze/Zie, Zir, Zirs.
Sie, Hir, Hirs.
E, Es, Em.
Xe, Xem, Xyr.

Will take some time to remember,
from what has been taught so many years.

They are out in the world.
They want to eat with us.
Not *they* as in many,
but *they* as in One.

Teach me and correct me with Grace.
Respect is recognition
that can be practiced both ways.

— T. Smith

X

"I had a dream," he said.

Five years later, Martin was dead—
marching from Selma to Montgomery.

Look at what they've done to me:
abomination,
genocide,
things he hoped he'd never see.

See, his spirit lives through me,
me and my bros,
when we're wearing the new 4s,
whipping the Benz with the 24s.

Don't say that's why we're poor.
Remember it was my heart that you tore.
You see the blood drip as I walk through the door—
or the aisle,
or the stage.

But the only time we walk down aisles
is when we're facing our newest case.

And we sag our pants,
and we kill each other—
our own blood brothers
and sisters.

The bullet just missed her,
and it was from you.

Martin said nonviolence and peace,
but I have to carry around a piece
just to survive in these streets.

Our complexion and our complexity—
it almost got the best of me.
Then I turned around and saw someone:
it was an angel next to me.

In a mirror
I was lost and gone,
I couldn't hear her.
Every time I watch the news
I see it clearer.

Emmett got lynched.
Rodney got beat.
Martin got shot.
Malcolm got shot.
Trayvon got hit—
and yet did he drop?

We can point fingers and look around,
but we all know when the sun goes down
we get to hear our favorite sound:

a gun,
a scream,
maybe some sirens in between.

Because they don't come anymore—
probably since we burned our block
ever since they shot Tyrone,
or Freddie,
or Michael.

It's an everlasting cycle.

We drop out of school.
We have no goals.
But we have goons—
cartoons that they imprint on our minds.

So our complex complexion,
our impression,
has an untold message.
But still, do we listen to what they tell us?

That one untaught lesson,
the bed that she never slept in—
but it was made for her.

Ever since they brought us here
we were considered poorer—
not poorer in mind,
but finances,
ambition and second chances,
young romances.

But we weren't taught right.
So she spread her legs one night.
He said that he was wrapped tight,
but that wasn't true.

Now all of her problems are multiplied by 2.

Is that what Martin marched for?
Is this what Rosa screamed for?

We say we're tired of losing this war,
but who's the enemy—
them or us?

We kill us more than them,
and that's why we cannot trust,
and why we cannot love.

"Let us not seek to satisfy our thirst for freedom
by drinking from the cup of bitterness and hatred."

This was stated.
We anticipated
the death of things we held sacred.
Maybe we should've waited.
These efforts can't be wasted.

For darkness is only overcome by light.
All the strife and plight,
we must continue this fight.

But how can we?

We have no leader.
We have no direction.
Please—
to everyone to help and spread this message.

For we are still limited by chains—
just chains of a different color.
It comes in gold now.
That's why he's not home now.
He's out here moving work
just so his mom won't have to go down.

He doesn't know his father.
Why do we even bother?
In court he said he needed the money
and that's why he shot her.

And he didn't care—
or maybe he didn't know.
We're so used to going with the flow.

And ignorance is bliss,
a sweet seducing kiss.
But in our world
it's eat or be ate,
get down or get laid,
spray them or be sprayed.

We took the blame for things we didn't do,
then we made points we couldn't prove.
Do the consequences get any worse?
What exactly do we have to lose?

Nothing.

Someone has to do something.
We fear the first step,
so we take what they give us:

drugs,
lust,
welfare,
bus,
minimum wage.

At this day and age,
we should have advanced,
but we're still stuck in a trance.

Don't hate me because I'm Black.
Pigment is nothing but a physical fact,
not the character that's intact.

Martin said don't stoop low enough to hate me.
So why do they chase me?

From Senegal to Florida,
longing for euphoria,
looking for the dividends of this formula.

When they had me in shackles,
bleeding profusely,
I started to pray—
but I use this term loosely.

When I was brought here,
my name wasn't Lucy.

My name was Chaka,
and I tried to align my chakras.
But instead we rather chop up
and bag it.

The things we need, we lack it.
It seems to be so tragic.
We need education,
not magic.
If I read a book,
would you match it?

They marched for miles—
frowns and smiles.
Was it worth their while?

Over bridges and through towns,
yet do the generations fall down?
You see the hands reach through the ground,
and you know that most of them are brown.

Harriet ran back for him,
took the loss,
got cracked for him.

But all we do is whip the bricks,
but not the ones our kids fit in.

They were born innocent—
a victim to what we created.
They look in the mirror
and see their reflection,
and I swear they hate it.

All he wanted to say was,
"Mama, I made it."

Then he was murdered in an alleyway.
In fact, it happened last Saturday.
We're worried about Freddie Mac and Sallie Mae—

but what about them shooting me?

They ask me what I see in my community.
I see dirty, dingy, unsuccess in this eulogy.

If Martin were here,
I'd ask him,
"What am I to do?"

Then he'd answer back and say,

*"Look in the mirror—
the change starts with you."*

— Kaamilah Diabaté

County Fair

The greatest illusion of all
is seeing these smiling faces down all these halls
ways away from civilization
or a place I would consider peaceful

Should be considered illegal
when presenting this story to other people—
deceitful,
even before we were old enough in age
to discover what was considered legal

An eagle
who is bald
a rare bird I'm trying to find because it's almost extinct
to make sense of everyone's emotions
and finding out what's distinct
what's really real?

Like me once believing in the Easter Bunny
but don't get me wrong
I'm still hunting for eggs trying to find clues
hopefully they're filled with sweet candy when I find them
or the candy might be bitter, outdated, or poison
much more of an annoyance than ivy

And losing sight of the path that's suppose to be taken
trying to be Mighty
will they ever see the right path that's likely unlikely?
a lot of you are cowards to doing the right thing
and that's me being nicely

Precisely—
that's me saying it politely
people want all the perks
without doing their homework and research
desperately in a panic and frantic for a savior to search
but reality hits them harder
than any Holy Ghost falsely consumed at any church

Just know it's not gonna work
seeing who you truly are
but you can't stand the sight of yourself
like standing in front of a mirror maze

And crime pays
and being a fraud is costly
I hope it was all worth it, being glossy and flossy
once you can't produce what others want any longer
you will be forgotten about

— A.W Jackson

if this is the last time i write a poem

if this is the last time i write a poem
if this is the last time i write a poem
i just want you all to know that my journey has been long,
it started with songs,
and when people did me wrong
now my spark for poetry is gone.

it's a feeling that i know a little too well,
i've written about suicide,
i've written about depression,
if i don't write anymore,
take my last poems
and use them as lessons,

if this is the last time i write a poem,
just know that i've never given up without a fight,
i've fought with all my might,
despite me beating all the times i've scarred my legs,
sitting on the shower floor,
i've watched me bleed, these tears i've shed
will water the seeds for my life's journey ahead

my spark for poetry is DEAD.

but i would be lying if i said that it was just poetry,
the way that life is doing me,
i swear it just ruined me,
since March of 2024
i've been begging life to let me go,
just loose your hold,
my heart turned cold,
the PAIN is "OH"
my purpose is old,
my mind is gone,

my body is numb,
i drink 'til i can't feel,
THIS LIFE CAN'T BE REAL

— Mari the Poet

Dead Poets Society

Bleed us lest our egos bruise
from droughts of praise and rave reviews,
though fleeting is our verse that shows
a flair that sheds our emperor's clothes.

Bleed us and exact our flesh
each drop and pound for words afresh,
as ransom though our voices die
in no-name graves where poets lie.

— Andrew Kouroupos

The Renegade

The hand that isn't raised often goes unseen,
hidden by harsh realities and broken dreams.

In a street life littered with rest in peace posters
and old candles for the youth,
it can be too much to handle.

Being hidden by bad grades and poor behavior—
but when you feel bad you want to scream:
it's not fair that you're living a nightmare
while everybody else lives their dreams.

It's not fair that things come easy to others,
but I always struggle.
At such a young age,
it's like the world I have to juggle.

When you have no role models,
just dead bodies and gold hollows.

But you can't wallow in your affliction,
because sensitivity is a conviction
when your patience coddles.

When you're lost with high expectations,
it's a hard pill to swallow.
Once you're labeled noncompliant,
it's hard to follow.

It's like having an open field
that's been fallowed.

You should've did it backwards
and took the pockets from the money,
so the money would spill
where junkies walk funny,
where the children play and pray,
where the children live and die.

Because there's stars on earth,
but there's no stars in the sky.

There's no food on the table.
There's no hope for the young.
Buying dreams isn't stable,
but I'll still buy one.

Because that's all I had—
a dream and some change.

I would dream for better days,
but nothing ever changed.

I would look for the light,
but darkness always came.

I would look for the love,
but the lies were never tamed.

A product of the environment,
the environment I became.

— Kaamilah Diabaté

Stolen Stories

Robbed of laughter
and the joy of being a child.

Robbed of sock hops
and introducing parents to first approved dates.

Robbed of figuring out what was liked,
and disliked.

Robbed of imagination and skills.

Robbed of knowing one's roots
and why all the sudden moves.

Robbed of memories that were never experienced,
and the opportunity to know which ones
could help future success.

Always watching other children play
and wondering what it's like.

Childhood friends growing up together,
sharing memories and dreams.

Robbed of having precious moments—
robbed of it all—everything.

— T. Smith

Jordan River

Trauma expressed through these little ones' faces,
through many different color races,
trying to strategically take many paces
so I can stay ahead of the game.
Like chess—
and I'm stressed,
because it's so dark but so beautiful all at the same time.
I feel sorry for those who are left behind.
I wish I could grab everyone's hand
and guide them through the finish line.
Dang… I wish I had more time.
Desperately trying to figure out solutions
to all the problems in the Dewey Decimal System,
while at the same time trying to inspire
and enhance the ecosystem.
Personalities and mannerisms
running through narrow bodies of water in a cramped space.
Then years go by and the bodies of water evaporate.
I didn't forget about the cool sensations
the bodies of water brought to my energy,
and warm experiences being added to my bucket list,
seeing connections and acceptance being shone from a distance.
And I smile—
maybe I should stay awhile.
Because not being present
will make things boil up like hot lava:
missing souls and characters sweet as guava,
being in a position that makes me realize
the importance of being father.
Improper punctuations
and misspelled words I have to correct,
so I start to erase all the errors that I see,
editing each sentence slowly,

until I'm satisfied and content
with the progress that was made.
And it's okay because I'm not perfect—
neither are they.

— A.W Jackson

My People

My people who are called by an answer to many names
choke on the Heimlich of society's blame.

No trees necessary for this innovative level of lynching;
generational roots gnarled by hate
spread their inheritance without flinching.

Brazen citizens no longer refrain
in their attempts at establishing white sheet domains,
boldly canvassing and enlisting recruits with similar opinions.
Zip/area codes yield to conglomerate dominion.

Industries encourage us to be Jim Crow 2.0 troopers,
as slurs become accepted bloopers.
Gender-neutral William O'Neals,
with cultural intentions camouflaged beneath bipartisan appeal.

Dismissing the remaining ancestral encyclopedias in our midst,
yet we choose to swap mother's milk
for the curdles of social media.

For over 400 years, we are accustomed to being the alien—
struggling to deal with the impact of our existence,
we are the original chameleons.

Often to our detriment, citizens report sightings of MFO's
(melanin foreign objects)
at schools, gas and train stations, restaurants, or in the woods:
colleges, malls, highways, corner stores, apartments,
and even walking or running in neighborhoods.

It's affirmative that action,
not abdication,
is what's required to empty the boiling antique pot of fighting crabs.
Every black-on-black crime keeps us in humanity's lab.

Hooded podiums designed
with more bondage in mind.
Chained melodies of commotion distort
the once sacred notes of liberty—
banning diverse lessons
while cleverly muting our voices in history.

Diasporic alarm clock frozen in the time zone of snooze.
Uncle Tom zombies feast on easily accessible, strange fruit.
Artificial hoodoo disguised as organic roots,
sipping and relishing on hyperbolic booze.

This global line dance we seem eager to learn
has a subconscious tempo meant to return
us to a captive, unnatural rhythm,
successfully silencing our genetic expression—
seemingly effortless steps of oppression.

Apparently, it's legal
to apply creative constitutional clauses against my people,
stealing our chronicles as the confederacy lulls us
with beats of assimilated latitude,
while still holding us hostage in covert servitude.

— Colette D. Jones

"How Is That Cool?"
Spoken Word Edition

You say I don't love you,
'cause I don't bend to disrespect.
But love don't mean letting you wreck
the house, the rules, the bond we protect.
You roll your eyes, slam doors, walk away,
thinking freedom means I can do it my way.
But tell me—
how is it cool to let your friends mock the ones
who put food in your mouth,
clothes on your back,
shelter around your head,
all while you act like love is dead?
We're good enough to pay the bills,
good enough to heal your ills,
good enough when you want or need—
but respect? That's not in the deal?
Nah. That's not real.
That's not love.
That's not right.
Scripture says clear—
"Children, obey your parents in the Lord, for this is right."
Honor is the law, not just a choice,
God said it Himself, not just my voice.
But you leave early morning,
come back deep in the night,
still I show love,
still I fight the good fight.
Yet I'm the bad guy—
the villain in your story,
while I'm holding up your world
quietly, without glory.
You think cool is doing whatever you feel,
but how is it cool

to break the hands that heal?
To despise the roof,
to curse the name,
to forget the Lord
who gave you your name?
I won't stop loving,
but I won't play the fool.
Respect is the rule—
so tell me, child,
how is this cool?

— Q Denise Masten

Chapter 3:
Echoes of Healing

Faith, God, survival, resilience, inner peace.

After the cries, the echoes are heard — prayers, songs, and questions that reverberate with hope. These poems sound like mending: where faith finds its echo, grief turns to light, and brokenness learns to heal.

Thank YOU, GOD!

GOD, YOU've brought me through a lot:
childhood sexual abuse,
abortion/miscarriages,
childbirth,
betrayal by friends
and loved ones,
cancer – more than once,
the inability to take care of myself – physically,
drug usage,
death of my parents, family members,
siblings, friends and acquaintances,
the disrespect of children,
rape,
the discovery of a sibling and
taking care of loved ones.

I've questioned YOU about it…
and YOU've showed me
that I can help others
through my experiences.

Though I wouldn't wish so much on one person…
YOU brought me through, each episode.
It's made me stronger,
able to support others and
unfortunately to know what the situation feels like.

I love YOU, GOD, because YOU
have been there through it all.
The experiences I hate to think about,
talk about, but do…
to help someone else.

YOU told me that YOU
would never leave me nor forsake me—
and YOU haven't.
Thank YOU, GOD.

YOU told me,
I'm more than a conqueror;
and I guess I am.
I know I wouldn't and couldn't
have gotten through all
I've been through without YOU.
THANK YOU, GOD.

— Graemme Denyce Boone

Use Me Lord

dear God,
this is the second letter that i've written to You.
i came here to say that i see Your people struggling—
it's hard to see
our mothers out here hustling.

so take their pain and put it all on me.
You're probably wondering, mari, what do you mean?
so i reply to You with watch and see.

God, come on.
the pain that my meme feels after losing her son—
give it all to me.
the way they feel after losing the one they love,
i know a little too well, so God watch and see.

i come to You as humble as i can.
You're the one with the plans,
but i'm willing to stop mine
if that means i can hold everybody's hand.

the people who have been mistreated, misled,
the teens who wish to be dead,
adults who've lost in their head—
take their pain and put it ALL on me.
take their thoughts and put them in mine.

i'm willing to sacrifice this body of mine
if that means that they'll feel Your presence.
God, i'm Your Job,
and i've learned Your lessons.
God, i'm Your Job,
i've gone through depression.

i've seen You work miracles,
so You're my obsession.
You saved me from dying,
all those nights i was crying,
the days i didn't feel like trying.
You took my hand and pulled me up.
i'm so glad i never gave up.

say to the people who say enough is enough,
please don't give up.

i'm here as a vessel.
i've watched You work miracles,
so take their pain and PUT IT ALL ON ME.

USE ME LORD, just WATCH AND SEE.
SEE HOW MANY PEOPLE WILL COME TO YOU.
EVERYTHING THAT I SAY IT WILL BE TRUE.
I KNOW IT WILL,
it's something i've been through.

the pain from my siblings—give it all to me.
take the baggage from my mom,
take the loads from my dad,
take the pain from their past
and put it all on me.

i promise i can handle it,
i promise i'll be careful with it,
just take it all and put it ALL ON ME.

God… i know You can hear me.
God, i know You can see me.

see me down on my knees.
God, i'm begging You please,
please give it all to me.

that baby who cries themself to sleep,
that baby who cuts their thighs and knees—
again i'm down on my knees and i'm begging You please.

my brother got down on one knee,
but he was betrayed.
take the pain from pyro's past,
and give it all to me.

take my pain from my baby,
and give it all to me.
i know she feels lost.
she made it to the top,
then her life suddenly stopped,
all because of a lie—
just give it all to me.

this is the end of my prayer.
i hope and pray that it will come true.
suicide isn't the answer,
so before they come to You,
i'm willing to take their pain,
because that's something You just can't undo.

— Mari the Poet

104

My Keeper

God is my Keeper,
even though the climb seems to get steeper.
I must keep looking up at the top,
because if I look down, I might drop.
I trust God to make it to my destination,
for a long time ago, I made reservation.

— Linda Crosby

Guided by Light

From the heavens,
a burst of light—
arms wide open,
embracing the sky.

I pray to You,
my Father above,
my voice rising
like wings in flight.

Guide me
through each moment,
through every breaking day.

I need You here,
in all I do,
in all I am becoming.

— Lisa Nicole Kennedy

Give Yourself Consent

Sometimes, you have to give yourself consent to be who you are,
So, step up, and become a star.
It's your turn to be on par.
Stop holding your own self back,
Don't derail stay on track.
Move out of your own way,
You have the cards to play.
So, get in the game, and stay.

— Linda Crosby

I Do Not Cry

I do not cry,
'cause you peacefully sleep—
free from pain and suffering,
I sigh with relief.

I do not cry,
my memories so sweet.
No more heartache nor mourn,
God's promises I keep.

I do not cry,
I celebrate my gift—
to be birthed by my Angel,
my heartbeat, you continue to lift.

I do not cry,
even tho our earthly time now cease.
I treasure our journey,
mother and daughter, my life complete.

I do not cry,
for I'll see you again,
restored with vigor and vim.
Paradise awaits you—
my heart and best friend.

— Marie Temple

Without Love

When my mind is near the steps of divinity,
how will I know it without you?

And when my sight is caught
in illusionary traps of nothingness,
how will I escape without you?

When the sun is still shining bright
on a cloudy day,
how will I show it without you?

And when those clouds have turned my sunny skies gray,
how will I keep warm without you?

When words fall upon me
with crushing force,
how will I not get hurt without you?

And when loneliness creeps in
with all my questions,
I remember, without a doubt,
I've found a love like no other in Christ.

And with a love so true, I know
…I am never without.

— Leroy Negus McDowell Jr.

i love you.

dear parents,
before i ever thought of writing you a poem,
it was a suicide letter.
so if you're listening to the poem
that means that life has gotten a little bit better.

i'm sorry;
give me some time to explain
why it was a suicide letter
and who's to blame.

at first it was you dad,
you were in and out of jail,
you left your kids to reminisce
and think about the way you were feeling in a cell,
all alone.

i know it hurts like hell,
but you just did wrong
and you had to do the consequence.
at the time it didn't make sense,
your kids didn't deserve the absence of their dad.
we were innocent.

you missed so many holidays and birthdays,
you didn't see your daughters on their worst days.
i just wanted the suicidal thoughts to come to an end.
y'all's baby wasn't happy—
i just wanted a kiss from my mama,
and a hug from my daddy.

but time flew by, i was happy for a while.
i got depressed and here's why.

mama:
it was once a time where you were my best friend,
i guess a lot of things do come to an end.
you started to become distant,
your babies wanted the old you back,
because your kids really missed it.

you held it down,
while dad was gone.
you were so independent,
you taught your babies to be strong.
but when daddy came home
you just started descending—
and that's why your oldest babies
were so angry.

i kept the pain to myself,
i didn't want y'all to feel it.
mama, when you seen the cuts on my legs
you said i'm like a lunatic.
sticks and stones didn't break my bones,
but your words really hurt.

i thought everybody's life would be better
if i was buried in the dirt.
but i thought to myself,
my uncle adrian would want to trade his six feet for hers.

now the roles switched.
i talk to my uncle from a grave,
praying and hoping
that he can hear the words from his khori.

i am MAD,
and i can't do my big one, old man.
i was living in hell,
the hell was my mind.

i was fighting tears every night,
PRAYING
to let it go away.

i was reading the book of Job
and i cried like he did.
i came across a verse,
i tried to pray,
but i shed a tear:
"God why am i here?"

i'm at church in the congregation,
pastor tries to lay hands,
my demons knuckle up.
the power of God takes over my life,
the holy spirituality says "what's up."

my flesh because weak,
i start crying because i can't even speak.
but i heard a voice say:
"baby give your all to me."

so i surrender to the king.
he takes me in as i am,
and he never judged.

when i was depressed for a while
i just called on him and i always felt loved.

from a person
who was struggling—
i'm telling you don't give up.
just give your life to God,
and i promise he will always show up.

— Mari the Poet

Snowflakes in the Dark

Today, oh! No longer am I bitter nor grim.
The peace that God brings now comes from within.
Life's beauty beams forth so vibrant, not dim—
in love with myself, my soulmate, and Him.

He is the one
who tenderly opened my heart.
Gentle words of endearment,
expressed sweetly from the start.

Whenever life seems to be pulling us apart,
it's down on my knees
begging discord to depart.

Like the delicate snowflake,
distinct in its beauty and shape,
are my prayers to My Father,
my Refuge and sheltered Escape.

The source of my strength
and my Provider of Grace.
His genuine love and most comforting care.
In presence is my dwelling and resting place.

Cascading through the darkness of night,
the moon is glistening, so warm and so bright.
Snowflakes fall gently, quietly and light,
bringing hope of the dawn very soon in sight.

— Marie Temple

Love's Idea

With great sovereignty, Love sat upon Eternity
calling out to beloved Peace,

"Come sit upon Eternity and bear witness
to the infinitude of Divine Mind
and the majesty of Creation
in all its possibility."

And there arose a great and beautiful Peace upon Eternity.
Then Love professed,

"Oh, how beautiful is Peace upon Eternity,
but where are the beloved I am in Peace,
for an idea has come from the darkness of Divine Mind."

Then from the ethers came forth the essence of Peace,
and Love found a great Wisdom and strong Will,
drunk in the bliss of matrimony.

"How wise is Wisdom and how strong is Will,
even unto the fires of pure perfection," Peace declared.

Then with a mighty thunder, Love announced,

"Because of the divinity within Peace,
I am perfected and have the Wisdom and Will to create."

So from that marriage sprung forth the essence of Truth,
and Love shined forth brilliance upon Peace,
ultimately astounded by the perfect oneness of Truth.

"Oh beloved Truth, I feel perfection in Peace
and the greatness of thy oneness with the One I Am,"
Love proclaimed.

And after 6 cycles of creating 9 stars
to govern the darkness of Divine Mind with Light,
Love formed an image to represent the marriage of
Wisdom and Will,
and declared it "Infinity."

Then Peace, from the magnitude of Light
that arrayed the deepest depths of Divine Mind,
gave birth to a most precious essence
and Love called out "Grace."

Then Love proclaimed,

"I Am made ANU in my oneness with Grace and Truth,
which shall be called such through all of infinity
and give light to fields of creation
that shall be called Patience."

And within 13 cycles of creating 7 Stars
to rule the ethers of Eternity, LOVE declared,

"For TRUTH and Grace shall conceive a great multitude of Stars
to give forth the Light of Creation
and that process is called Time.
All the great stars shall be birthed in Patience.

The Children of a perfected Love, this great multitude shall be,
and Truth shall be called their Father—
always serving as an eternal guiding light upon Eternity,
always shining forth the essence of great Wisdom
and strong Will,"
Love proclaimed.

Love went on declaring,

"Then in oneness, Truth shall place each upon the breast of Grace
to be nourished by the essence I am
until I have made the great multitude call her Mother."

And Love ended this sovereign declaration with,

"And in that oneness will come the greatest Light,
formed by the great magnitude and in alignment of all the stars.
Anu Wisdom and Anu Will shall be born,
and all shall call it Love's Idea."

And so it is!

— Leroy Negus McDowell Jr.

More Skin In The Game

I don't have to put more skin in the game,
because He knows my name.
And that's not about bragging or boasting.
It is about God, Who, I am toasting.
Cheers!

— Linda Crosby

God, I Have a Question

I was told at a young age
to never question you.
But also I know we have relationship,
so I have a few.

God, I know you love me, but why?
When the people who follow you say
I'm a disgrace in your eye.

Yet you so show me grace and mercy
every day my head and eyes lift up.
Your spirit of love and joy
fills my eternal cup.

God, why is it the world is against me
but claims you in their condemnation?
I get confused by them all,
even the ones through spiritual recommendation.

Yet I still follow only your way.
But times I'm conflicted—
I just want to be free
and unrestricted.

Understanding rules and repercussions is standard,
but even when I followed those protocols
I still got slandered.

Yet I never wanted to ask you these things,
however here I am.
I don't want to anger you
nor feel emotionally damned.

I see these questions are more concerns
than what I thought.
Seeking you was the best thing
I could have ever sought.

I know I'm not the only one
with these feelings.
These concerns are in the journey
to personal healing.

I know your daily work with me
shows your love for me
and divine suggestions.

Yet and still—
in all relationships
we have questions.

— Sean Martin

The Face of My Mother

As I glanced into the mirror
in disbelief and terror,
I saw the face of my mother.

Blackened eyes, shut ever so tight—
only darkness within my sight.
I wore the face of my mother.

How could life repeat itself?
Why, dear God, had no self-worth?
Behold the face of my mother.

Thy inherit shame and guilt,
the cloak passed down, so I foolishly took.
Unfold the face of my mother.

Childishly, I stepped into place,
to put on the apron of disgrace—
and bore the face of my mother.

Sons and daughters release the blame,
undoubtedly chose to claim.
Retreat from the face of my mother.

Jah has brought us both to peace.
No longer shall either of us weep.
Reframed is the face of my mother.

— Marie Temple

On Purpose for Purpose

All that's happened in your life is for a reason.
All the ins and outs throughout the seasons.
Yes, it hurts. You may have fears and questions—
all these situations are teachable lessons.

In life, we go through ebbs and flows.
You will learn all but God only knows.
Never give up because things are not going your way.
But also understand that tomorrow is not promised,
so never worry about the bad days.

Look over and focus on your beyond.
That's how you become centered
and create unbreakable bonds.

You will overcome just by having joy in your heart.
Also, your love for self will not depart.

Stand tall through your ordeal, whether it's unsure.
That's how you're letting the universe know
that you are built to endure.

You are loved, you are not alone.
Your testimony is made to help
those that you know and those that are unknown.

These words you are reading are only to encourage,
so don't beat yourself and feel discouraged.

Get up and keep pressing.
Remember, like before, this is all a lesson.

This is all for service,
because your story is written.
And you are here on purpose for a purpose.

— Sean Martin

A Plea for Peace and Forgiveness

And from many
Fear is offered in the face of Forgiveness.

And with this
a stone of ignorance is cast
across the still Waters of Peace.

Then low sails Forgiveness
into the depths of infinity.

And upon the mountain tops of wisdom
forgiveness is seen.

Then in comes the clouds of distraction
to block the Clear View of True Perception.

And from that point
Forgiveness begins to wait
until Peace takes flight.

Then into the heavens of Love,
Forgiveness sets sight.

That day will be bright
when Forgiveness goes away.

And in that day
many will search for Peace,
but Forgiveness will have left its way
and found another home for Peace,
far, far away.

— Leroy Negus McDowell Jr.

It's Personal

I've been tested,
I'm hoping my dreams will be manifested.

Putting in blood, sweat, and tears into what I desire,
waiting for what's promised to me and acquired.

My heart is pacing and racing for the reward.
My praise and my faith unto, to you Lord, is on one accord.

God, I'm being patient and keeping my sanity,
yet through this process, You are restoring my humanity.

My strength comes from knowing
You are making all things connect together.
I'll continue to praise You still
in all the four seasons of weather.

The praise I give is never wavering and will not question
Every time I close my eyes
I see the blessings that are predestined.

So tangible I feel them close to me,
to grab and hold with my hands.
As I wait, I won't drift away—
I'll continue to stand.

I am human, so my feelings will tend to shift from time to time.
Day to day, I truly believe victory is and shall be mine.

In this place I'm alone, but I know of Your presence,
and that keeps my heart filled with effervescence.

Being content in the now is the test I'm faced with,
knowing I'm steps away from a testimony
and knowing it's not a myth.

This yearn inside my heart won't turn,
and I know that this flame will continue to burn—
until I receive,
that I'll without a shadow of a doubt to believe.

Knowing this is for me to strengthen me as an individual
this is all for His glory which makes it personal.

— Sean Martin

Healing

When tears hit the ground, flowers grow
Thru the process of healing many certainly will flow

Time and remembrance can become a formidable foe
It will take all or at least a piece of your divine glow

Such elusiveness when it's not clear which way to go
For most, if completion does come, it does so quite slow

I can stand upon these words
for this I personally know

The process could be ongoing, at times never complete
Becoming a daily struggle to not fall victim to defeat

This too, you can overcome; this too you can beat
Never allow the going thru to render your willpower obsolete

Adverse conditions are where the person you think you are,
and the person you truly are,
come to meet

— Watson John

Chapter 4:
Ballads of Love

Romance, intimacy, connection, friendship, family bonds.

Love sings in many registers — tender, fierce, fragile, and unyielding. These ballads carry their melodies: confessions, heartbreaks, and vows, each note reminding us that love is not only felt — it is written, sung, and remembered.

Corner of Everlasting

I would crawl through glass,
walk through fire,
ice that burns,
travel past floating lilies,
weeping trees that echo my pain—

all just to reach you,
to whisper the words my heart cannot hold,
to tell you, again and again,
that I love you.

And there,
at the corner of everlasting,
where sorrow bends into light,
I will find you waiting,
and love will remain.

— Lisa Nicole Kennedy

Future Love

If two wrongs don't make a right
then tell me why I'm here with you.
We flow like two steams intersecting into an ocean.
They say opposites attract,
but our bond is stronger than two magnets.

Bad boy, nice guy, geek, pretty boy, player, mamma's boy, jock—
No labels can describe you.

Some may say I'm head over heels, knees buckle Nancy, love at
first sight,
so blind I can't see straight, whipped woman that I am.
But all I see are your kind eyes, your giving heart, your sexy
smirk,
your intelligence, your zest for life and living...

Am I wrong to only notice that?

I also hate when you're right and I'm wrong.
I hate when you beat me in chess.
I hate that you know me so well, sometimes you use it for playful
game.
I hate that you wear that same ol' hat every day.
I hate that sound you make when you're excited,
on the brink of some genius moment.

I also hate when you're gone,
even when you make me mad and I want you to leave...
You stay.

I also hate that you know my tickle spot...
You never let go.

I can't stand when we have playful competitions,
especially with sports, because most times you try to cheat,
figuring out my strategy.

When I make mistakes it's hard for me to admit it to you—
not because I'm scared, but because I don't want to see
your *I told you so* face.
I'm hard headed and stubborn,
but you always seem to break that barrier with one kiss and one
touch.

I am overwhelmed and overjoyed with gladness that I have you in
my life.
I am so deeply in love with you,
your happiness has become more important than my own.

So I write all these feelings down,
and hopefully one day you will read this.

For all the future lovers out there,
may you find the very things you need in someone.

— Meagan C. Jefferson

His Voice

was like reverent silence in a rushing storm,
a calming stillness, gentle wade on an ocean shore.
We were friends with a shared fascination
for long walks and conceptual conversations.
But for me it was the sound of his sultry "hello"
mellowing my uncertainties, making home in my soul.
It was white noise to my REM,
a trancing hum of a ceiling fan,
a warming sensation of a first sip,
like daydreaming of a long-awaited first kiss.
I'd gather many questions
just to hear him speak
rhythms of elegance.
Like prayer as Communion
touched my lips.
He'd caress my ear
with subtle mentions
of adoration, admiration.
"Invaluable," he said.
My friendship was invaluable to him.
His stature: broad-shouldered, tall
gently spoken man
with an audacious vernacular
that just so happened
to soothe the slightest fractures
of my mind.
His voice was one of a kind.
And I... I was under his spell.

— Sharese Simone

BLACK ROSE

BLACK ROSE
Definitive of a unique prism,
a carnation that flows red, burgundy,
and a purplish coterie of prismatic colors:
ominously a

BLACK ROSE
How dare you choose to glow, grow, and gravitate
with deep, black velvety petals
in the wind and rains of life.

Permeated to blossom—
blossoming to the beat of your own drum
that echoes differently.
Their perception is your perfection.

BLACK ROSE
Unhinged doors open;
one's gait, disposition, and poise are demure;
trailblazing the torch unchartered, uncensored, and unapologetically
breaking the glass ceiling—
exhausted from traditional stigma:
manifesting self-gentrifying;
strength and seduction tutorial of a successful flower.

BLACK ROSE
Who, what, where, and how it cultivates:
blueprint drawn not to scale;
reaping what you sow.

The ambience of a spiritually divine ambrosia;
scent of an anointed fragrance
with a sprinkle of educated, whimsical petals.

Talking to God for His permission,
and God whispered, "you go La Rose Femme"
as I ponder the question—
Who am I?

BLACK ROSE

— Ruth Redmond

Love Language

Love can be blind;
Love can be bold;
Love can be forgiven,
yet Love can unfold.

Inward and outward signs for attention/affection:
riding a Love rollercoaster.

Arts of expression incorporating a nostalgic scenery.
Pondering, how did this happen?

Puberty crept into the night,
bringing along unannounced endorphins—
spewing into adulthood, judging in plain sight.

Love Language

It takes two to unify but one to unite,
allocating a piece to become one's peace
amid this emotional fight.

Strolling hand in hand, vibrations heavy within.
Seductress visions of a honey, roasted, cocoa butter skin—
rubbing, caressing from the top of your head
down to your shin.

Love Language

Unselfishly sharing and comparing thoughts and dreams.
Past, present, and future endeavors gleam.
Collaboratively collecting an algorithm of a euphoric high,
secrets unfold as doves do cry.

Then evening falls,
as one gazes out the window while cuddling a glass of wine in hand.
Soft, sexy music echoes in the background,
dreaming life is so grand.

Shiny, silky silhouettes dancing widespread,
full of giddy and glee—
as metaphoric quotes recite from within me.

The moon is surrounded by cosmic stars,
as overnight forecasts of emotions and memoirs fall.

Then here comes the sun,
basking the question—was it all a dream
or simply love life's meme?

Love Language

— Ruth Redmond

What Is Love

Love is a feeling that symbolizes warm emotions;
it is a beautiful woven thread filled with boundless creativity.
Love is like a secret language that is not always easily explained
and does not need words to make sense.

Love is a language of its own,
a blend of integrity, loyalty, and magical mystery
that are alluring and alive.
Love is like a mixtape filled with dancing, laughter,
and enchanting, mysterious whispers of honesty,
loyalty, elegance, grace, and compassion.
Love creates a place of peace,
intertwined with harmony, and tenderness.

Love is an intense feeling, deep affection,
and genuine connections,
with spontaneous moments shared between two people,
through a mutual understanding.
It is the essence of unique qualities
and the building block of strong feelings.

Love is a bond that listens, provides,
and supports unconditionally.
Love is like a solid rock with a dash of prayers
and a dusting of beautiful vibes.

Love is all about honest conversations, sincere moments,
and no hidden agendas.
Love is like a romantic sunset shared between two beautiful souls,
a rare sense of loyalty, and a promise to heal together.

Love has the desire to really listen
and contains a heart that gives without expecting in return.
Love is about insignificant sacrifices and huge gestures,

appreciation, respect, and endless support.
Love is a keeper of promises and a courageous protector.

But above all,
love has no bounds,
and it is that warm and comfortable place
where you feel safe.

— T. A. Broady

Raven's Cry

I can hear the raven's cry
echoing on the hill,
where nothing but madness
and silence remain.

Empty days seep
into colder nights,
the phantom scent of us
still lingers—
where we once made love,
where gold once glowed,
a paradise now turned
mysteriously dark.

The last smile we shared
is burned into memory,
a flame that will not fade.

You are gone,
yet my mind plays tricks—
in shadows,
in whispers,
I swear somehow
I still touched you.

— Lisa Nicole Kennedy

Without A Doubt, I Say

You walked in slow, with a sexy sideways grin,
Wearing mischief that smelled of brown sugar and sin.

You asked, "Is this seat taken, miss?"
I sipped my drink and blew a small kiss.

Your charm was loud, your shirt was sexy and bright,
But somehow… still, you wore it right.

I said, "You think you've got a shot?"
You winked. "Definitely—not?"

We danced like we were on a tipsy carnival ride,
My heels betrayed me—twice, I think—
But you kept me close and held on tightly to my side.

You caught me both times as I slipped,
You dipped me, oh so smooth,
Our moves, very cleverly hidden,
So that no one else would see our missing groove.

"You like me," you said, all proud and bold,
As if your smile was made of gold.

I rolled my eyes, but couldn't leave—
Because, well…
Unquestionably, you just might be
The special one for me.

— T. A. Broady

I AM

Be in Faith   Live the Faith   Walk with Faith.

Psychedelic forum of mixed emotions—
buoyant, flamboyant, resilience and some.
The ups and downs of unwanted, unfavored phases;
highs and lows of unchartered stages:
fight or flight—
fear or persevere.

Questions to embrace this pink burden that somehow found
me—
the uninvited guest messing with my breast.

Hell yea! With pride, prejudice, and conviction: **I AM.**

Head hurts, body aches, IV's drips of confusion,
unyielding side effects from piercing and probing skin.
To be a striver, thriver, transcending goddess: **I AM.**

Pre, post, and future terms of endearment—
a pink love letter journals the before and after;
the pros and cons;
the why me to why not me—
channeling the pathway in becoming the CEO of one's life fully:
I AM.

In that competitive ring,
she proudly donned the pink boxing gloves and accepts what
brings—
a wounded soldier to a warrior soldier,
marching to my own beat.

Sashaying the new look—
grinning from ear to ear,
tattoo nipples represent my conquest cheer.
I stand tall—deformity and all: **I AM.**

Tears flow, cry me a river,
but it's alright and it's okay—perplexed human nature.

God said Noah did not build an ark in one day,
so with that said—what comes my way.

Sound the alarm, the ringing, clinking the bell that ends,
but accepting a new era begins.

Solstice sounds of healing and peace.
Joy comes in the morning as the assignment is finally at ease.

I may not look the part
because I am the part.

I AM A BREAST CANCER SURVIVOR.

— Ruth Redmond

Black Love Is

Black love is family,
Acceptance,
Strength,
Protection and Loyalty.

Black love is—
Kindness,
Consistent.
It is Constant.
It is Unconditional.

Black love is—
Intimacy,
Complimentary.
It is selfless.

Black love is hearing music and your favorite song while remi-
niscing.
Black love is dancing close,
sharing your space,
and magical moments with someone significant to you.

Black love is remembering your grandparents,
Sunday dinners, soul food, and Saturday morning chores—
at the same time, music playing in the background.

Black love is remembering watching Soul Train on Saturdays,
dancing down the Soul Train line with your friends and family.
Watching Good Times, The Jeffersons, and What's Happening
and seeing people on TV looking like you.

Black love is remembering road trips to nowhere,
packing snacks—fried chicken, white bread, and Big K sodas—
trips to the park, family reunions, cousin bonds, and pinky swears.

Black love is moonlight walks by the lake,
on the beach, or in the park,
while sharing intimate secrets and life dreams.

Black love is the bond you share with childhood friends—
lasting friendships,
laughing hysterically while reminiscing
over memories from your village, your hometown,
and your circle of friends.

Black love is that early morning check-in,
that quick text,
or that 2-minute phone call
that turns into 2 hours
as you talk about current events, family, and life.

Black love recognizes that our Black kings are amazing,
even in a world that unfortunately paints them in a view
that makes them second-guess who and what they are.

Black love is a beautiful queen strolling past
in her elegant fashion—
fresh, natural hairstyles, big hoop or wooden earrings,
dewy fresh skin,
and smelling like fresh fruit and berries.

Black love is irresistible and irreplaceable.
Black love is many things: traditions, memories, values, ideas,
and dreams.
But most of all, Black love is a strong sense of pride and belong-
ing.

Black love is family!

— T. A. Broady

Final Goodbye (A Love Letter)

NPM 1/30
I can't stay
Feeling like I'm in the way
Blocking the entrance to the space
Once held as mine
Now time has shown
What we had has grown
Cold
Like arctic waves against frozen shores
We are no more
Mere vapors of what was
Evaporating into an abyss of forgotteness
I won't stay
Where my presence isn't appreciated
In a place where my caring isn't reciprocated
Unvalued like counterfeit currency
Refused the urgency that my love requires
Our time has expired
So I step aside to let you do you

I bid adieu

— Ren

Dear Yvette

Her life spun faster than she did on the pole—
except there she had control.

Touched at 10,
her introduction to love,
innocence lost before it was found.

A change came as soon as her "uncle" did.

A tisket,
a tasket,
he put change in her basket—
and the almighty dollar became her man.

You see,
she would grin for Grant,
freak for Franklin,
laugh at Lincoln.

Moved from dope boys, hustlers, and ballers
without thinking.

Her mind on the money,
their money on her mind,
never seeing faces—only dollar signs.

Intimate encounters minus desire,
as she gave her soul away,
leaving pieces of herself
on stages,
while scribing her pain on pages.

The only place she ever cried
was when she realized that she died
before she ever began to live.

— Ren

The Mathematics of Love

I only wanted to love 1

You decided that you needed 2

The more the merrier

A 3 way love affair

A betrayal my multiple broken heart

Could not 4get

5 years instantly subtracted from me

I still remember the way he smiled at me

Adding insult to injury

As my 6th sense told me he was more than "just" a friend

Divided by my heart and mind

I designed my end

Took you back and trips to 7th heaven ensued

Along with promises that only held a fraction of truth

The 8-minute voicemail brought me back to reality

Confirming that our situation was a true fatality

Plunging me through the 9 circles of hell

But to no avail I fell

Victim

Broke all 10 Commandments for the sake of love

Now I find no solace in God due to my emotional sin

Left with just a percentage within

— Ren

Chapter 5:
Rhythms of Vision

Creativity, poetry, imagination, future dreams,
the writer's purpose.

The poet's pen is blueprint and prophecy, shaping new worlds, wrestling with truth, and insisting on legacy. Here it becomes an instrument — moving in beats, riffs, and visions, playful and bold. Even when voices falter, the words remain — alive, defiant, and enduring.

Intro: Set My Space

Peace and Love...
I send you and your family
an abundance of ease, joy, and wellness.

These are love messages from me to me,
expressions of my aggressions channeled in
different sessions, before I even got the chance to
digress them.

Learning the lesson that I am the conduit,
being the reflection you need, to speak up freely.

I ask if you have the capacity to do so to softly put
your right hand on your heart and your left hand on
your stomach…

To lock into this present moment,
think of a flower that represents you best.
All while being mindful of your breath…

Inhale deeply through your nose...
Exhale slowly through your mouth...
Being reminded of your flower essence.

Even if it has been a while,
this is the perfect time to smile.
Because I see Rose, I hear you Tulips,
I feel you Lavender, I smell you Baby's Breath,
I remember you Lillies,
I know you Gerber Daisy.

...now that I have your attention,
take my hand to pick up on the mentions
that will be presented...

— Tunisia RaWanda

Harmony Retreat

It's a universal meeting for everyone in America to meet
So be there at 3 PM
so that gives everyone enough time to eat

This isn't an entreat
but instead a happy hour
where alcohol isn't allowed
and we will be meeting somewhere with a lot of land

Maybe Boulder
Somewhere surrounded by nature's vivid grass and trees
much fresher than lemon squeeze

In walking distance there would be a large body of chairs
where we can all sit and converse
where we would take all of our ideas, themes, and solutions and
disperse
back to what we all would consider home

The best teachers in the world are those who listen
doesn't matter your position
because we can all learn something new

We would all learn a new language that day
and that would be the cure for hate

We would run for cover from all the foolish things and thoughts
that poisoned our brains

Unspoken law—
we would all eliminate the negative voices from the past
that positive and loving energy would get broadcast
to every person, even if you know them or not

For mysterious reasons we were all silent
taken in a moment of peace
then the next moment we released
all the hate we had at this crowded table

So we would scoot over
so love can have some room to sit

Then I woke up from a beautiful vision
and got instantly sad… truthfully, I have to admit
would a moment like this ever really exist?

— A.W Jackson

Blueprint of My Sky

I dream in colors the world has not named,
shades stitched from hope and half-lit mornings,
threads of gold pulled from the edge of tomorrow,
woven into a map I carry in my chest.

I dream of voices that heal instead of harm,
of hands that reach without hesitation,
of streets that hum with kindness
the way summer hums with bees.

I dream of art spilling from my fingertips,
letters and lines like lanterns on the water,
guiding strangers to something familiar—
a truth they forgot they knew.

I dream of roots deep enough to hold me steady
and wings wide enough to take me anywhere,
of laughter that echoes in rooms I have yet to enter,
of a love that feels like a long-awaited home.

Some dreams are quiet,
like a garden waiting for rain.
Some roar like oceans in my veins.
But all of them—
every single one—
is stitched into the blueprint of my sky.

— Amy Michelle Kennedy

My ARTerial Vein

Creative and
beautiful
attached to my Aorta
ART
A purpose in my life
No mistakes
No rules
No limits
Just a story
branching from me
to you
ART
a source of oxygen
Breath
Life
Purpose
My ARTerial vein
ART

— Aryianna Edmond

Man's Best Friend

A sidekick sent from heaven
Loyal and
Loving
Always there with a tail wagging
or a wet kiss.
My best friend.
Sent here to complete a family.
The watcher,
the protector,
the missing piece.
Proof that love is not conditional
but treats and belly rubs
are always welcome.
God's promise that His love
is sometimes disguised as
a furry friend.

— Aryianna Edmond

NOUNS

Looks like we're living in a time when folks don't know
how to properly address each other
They're disrespectful
They spew downright ig'nant shit from their mouths
And have seemingly forgotten that we're all human beings
I have a suggestion that can safely be used for all

NOUN

It's one of the only "N-words" that should ever be used
when addressing Black people

NOUN

It's all encompassing:
Hey, look at that noun over there!
All nouns deserve respect!
I'm a noun, and so are you!

NOUN

How about that?
Is that easy enough?
Does that break it down in the terms simple enough
for you to understand how to properly address others?

I'm a noun, you're a noun, we're all nouns!

Can you get with that?
Try it out
And maybe the empathy
The compassion
The understanding
The respect

For others
Will guide our words
Our thoughts
Our attitudes
And our actions toward each other

Because we're all nouns!

Did it slip your mind that you're one, too?

— Buddah Desmond

'EDUMACATION'

Settled.
Believing it's cool to be drawn into the crowd—
for the show off—just to belong!

Convinced that peers have it all worked out,
that hanging out in school hallways is the priority.
Convinced that in-class learning is boring,
irrelevant,
not at all a necessity.

They tell themselves and everyone else close enough to hear…
"There's nothing worth learning in those 'edumacation' rooms out
there!"

Is this mindset reigning in our communities,
mounting concerns in the hearts of the innocent,
no matter the age, size, or color?

Breaking News tell of in-store designer stuff
looted and loaded—raided for profit—
one way or another.

Running from the truth,
running wildly,
blinded in a spiraling frenzy,
refusing to trust how truth and abundance aligned
could actually be.

"There's nothing worth learning in those 'edumacation' rooms out
there!"
is what I keep hearing,
creating a disturbance deep inside of me.

Do you not know who you are?
Yes—You—Sistah-Gurll!

You are far more valuable
than the charm fantasy creates.

In real time,
in earth-bound situations,
your carriage commands pause.
Unbeknownst perhaps—Queen—
you were stacked for a righteous cause!!

Your body is a sacred vessel,
created to be cherished,
and not sex-trafficked.

Your body is first yours
to respect and honor;
with aim—excellence of purpose,
pursuit of higher ground.

Creator-God never intended life
to be lived without a sound mind.
Never was the plan alienation
from the wealth intended for you to find.

There can be no continuance of the human family
in the absence of you!

Your richness and love capacity
deposits in every breath-wish you issue.

What was told or shown to you
outside of truth, is a lie.
Consider it rubbish,
Leave it behind!

— Mildred M. Stokes

Pocket

A-Tisket, A-Tasket,
playing games, essentially a bet,
without fear of gratitude, or debt.

Hickory, Dickory, dock,
they holler, scream, and mock,
always ready, to lock or rock.

Eeny, meeny, miny, moe,
fighting fair, without hearing no,
pressing hard, always on the go.

A limited month is given,
hoping and wishing, it's Unforgiven,
without regard to the inconstant cleft, or riven.

Instead, cheer, no boos or jeers,
a celebration of love over fears.

Give a metaphorical socket, moving faster than a rocket,
now placing, a wocket in your pocket.

— Meagan C. Jefferson

Two-Stepping Between Power + Evil

Creating a nation in your own image
With crippling effects here and abroad
The detriment to what and to whom is of
little care or consequence
You'd watch this place crumble piece by piece
And probably will even delight in the lives
destroyed in its process
As long as no one comes above thee
Cherishing nothing other than loyalty
Czar, King Oligarch, Ruler of All…

They say power will make you do things
They say power will make you do some things
They say power will make you do many things

Damn shame how much damage and suffering
occurs at the hands of the inhumane
two-stepping between power and evil
Damn shame they're still winning while
two-stepping between power and evil
Damn shame how much we have to lose
while they're politricking and
two-stepping between power and evil

As history has proven, periods such as these never last
Imagine their disbelief when their
heartless, rhythmless reign ends
And the takeover by a righteous regime
truly for the people begins

In the glorious spirit of Stacey Abrams and the legendary
brothers James Weldon Johnson and John Rosamond Johnson,
we must *resist, persist, and insist till victowry is won.*

— Buddah Desmond

160

Stuck

A shell of a man.
Sinks into the sand.
Looking hollow and bland.
He's been broken and slammed.
Still he shines all he can.
To hide tears in his hand.
While he sinks like it's planned.
Cause he feels like he's damned.

— N.F.G.

God Loves Us Too

We are an amalgam of our ancestors
Perfect imperfections
Beautiful and intelligent
Equal to any race
From daylight to darkness
God wraps his love around us

— Nicole Lanier Montez

Engaged

His heart is too big for his spine.
And his mind is too cold for his heart.
Dissecting the world's design.
As it chokes him and rips him apart.

— N.F.G.

Poetic Thoughts Pt. 1: The Understanding

just as i am

people can love me
just as i am.
people can hate me
for who i be.

no matter their prophecy,
there is nothing

they can say,
there is nothing
they can do
that will stop me.

this is my reality,
this is my destiny,
this is what
God has for me.

this is Lee III.
i never imagined
i would be blind
by the age of 23,
but still i am happy,
still i am grateful to thee.

love me just as i am,
not for who i use to be,
not for who i will be.

love me just for me,
just as i am.

i am giving me to u,
this is me completely.
this is not
a perception of me,
this is me honest,
this is me true.

i don't give a damn
if people don't like it.
this is me,
just as i am.

No power like black power.
Hey black sista,
don't you know
that there is…

— Poetic Messiah Willie James Lee, III

Everlasting

Every year around this time he removes eight boxes from the
basement
        - carefully placing the contents on
Prior to leaving
        - he gives himself a once-over in the mirror
Every little step toward his destination
        - brings him back to first times

Melodies and lyrics play in his mind
Decades ago, family and friends gathered and wished them well
Today, he is gathered together with a weeping willow tree, red
rose bushes, chrysanthemums, and birds
Kneeling on his brides' grave he pledges his everlasting love

— Nicole Lanier Montez

The Rhythm

A lyrical rhyme
Is spiritual divine
Its a gift and a sign
That will lift you and shine
It will show you the way
The truth and the light
It will grow you each day
And improve you each night
It will flow from your soul
To The goal in your sight
It will glow from your roll
Control and ignite

— N.F.G.

Oath of the Silent

Confessions wrapped in lessons,
full of impressions,
of objects for affection.

Rooted in blame,
embarrassed and ashamed,
with nothing to keep sane.

Laughing through pain,
searching for fame,
as if it's a game,
with endless aim.

Enemies surrounding,
not loosening its grip,
waiting for loose and unattended flesh to rip.

Crying out for help,
silent tears,
invisible hopes,
to cover up fears.

Peace or understanding is what naysayers ridicule and chuckle
over,
knowing their plight is to cover up notions they can devour,
by forcibly placing attention on delusions of grandeur.

Persistence, patience, and perseverance are virtues one should
hold near and dear,
always reaching for goals and dreams,
professing spiritual awakenings of growth,
to heal wounds,
blocking its shine.

Oppressed, shunned, and hushed for uttering injustices,
these silent and afflicted personages
rise towards opposition,
tearing down its cast of shadows,
masking as giants.

Division and separation must terminate,
replacing with unity and love,
giving strength to those who suffer
through isolation and alienation.

A reinvigorated decree of liberation
now grants opportunity to recently reformed people,
willing to harness the responsibility
to be, no longer silent.

— Meagan C. Jefferson

Still Making a Difference

In a world of tech, she stands tall
A pencil with a disability, defying it all
Though her grip may be weak and her lines may be faint
She refuses to let her limitations taint
With determination in her graphite core
She writes stories, and planning for more
Her lead may be broken, but her spirit is strong
As she proves to the world she still belongs In a digital age, she
may seem out of place
But she makes her mark with grace and grace
Her strokes may not be pixel perfect
But her words and ideas are truly worth it
For in a world of screens and clicks
She reminds us to slow down and fix
Our eyes of the people our hands on the pan
Sometimes on paper is where we must begin
So let her inspire us all
A pencil with a disability standing
Before she shows no matter our flaws
We can still make a difference even with pencil and pause

— Q Denise Masten

Midnight Crown

Inside a lovely wooden shrine,
There was a crown, darker than the night sky.
It spoke to the girl standing outside,
"Raise me as your helm to save yourself."

"Are you some sort of god?"
The girl asked tentatively.
"What have I done to deserve your charity?
And what if you end up hating me?"

The crown glimmered and said,
"Even so, before that day comes,
I'd be honored with the privilege
To be worn by you.

"For, as a god, it is my job,
 To raise you to your feet.
 Let us escape our solemn solitudes,
 And together, let us be free."

— Jada Ware

Inspiration

The Midnight Crown was inspired by the English cover of *The Dream the Doll Girl Dreamed* by SirHamnet. It is the story of a doll who loves her creator and views him as a god. The human man denies this and tries to persuade her against loving him.

While listening to the song, I thought: *"Instead of a doll and a human man, what if there was a talking crown and a human girl?"* Each stanza was meant to be a parallel to certain parts of the song.

- In the song, the girl represents love and kindness, while the man represents humanity.

- In the poem, the girl represents humanity's hopelessness, and the crown represents the hope and guidance a person needs to continue living.

B.A.Ū.M

I know myself to be a Beautiful Sunflower Soul.
Whose trūth is being told through her Sunshine Glow.
Standing bold, ascending into her higher flow.

This is a reminder to you...
That everything you do affects your hair too…

So please don't be confused by my lounging...
This is my definition of grounding.
It is all encompassing to the crowning of my hair...
My mind, my body and my soul.

Trūth be told, that's the page they ripped out.
And put into a fold.
Because it's the very thing that makes our hair and our souls grow.

Nevertheless, I digress.
Yet...
When it comes to braids you see...
This is how I channel my ancestral frequency.

Sometimes I have thoughtful thoughts.
That create vicious mistakes.
Finding out it created the space for equilibria...
My unique cosmic criteria.

So I have been given consent to show up like this...
Regardless of everybody else's two cents.
It's been stuck all up in me.
Until I gave permission to the kid in me,
to just be young, wild and free.

Braiding free...
As they whip back and forth like the essence of a willow tree.
Cause operating in this creativity...
Reminds me of who my ancestors be,
before that thang called slavery.

My consciousness be in the sixth dimension.
Creating these baum distinctions of excellence.
And I'm not talking about bomb...
Like that song "Bombs over Baghdad."
I'm talking about baum.
B - A - Ū - M.
Because I am trūly rooted like the thickest part of the tree.
If you look up the definition
to the word "baum," that's what it means,
You see...

That's why I'm ok with being an Outkast.
The Universe got my back like chiroprac.
Sprinkling my effect in all my alignments.

Matter fact she always helping me be bold.
To channel my remold soul.
To keep my crown polished in gold.
Because once upon a time our hair was pimped out,
by white international players.
A known silent code...

To now know that my crown only folds...
When I replant my soiled soul into my primogenitors up hold.
For me to receive the abundance ten fold.
And pass that jaunt down this newly built...
Underground railroad.

Welcome to the Yellow Brick Road...
Of no longer being Tressed Oūt.
This spill is the very reason why I left the "S" out.
Because you and I know that our hair has always been the clout.

To all the beautiful flowers in this space to be,
currently reading...
Let this be the reflection you need, to turn up your authenticity...
Respectfully of course.

I know myself to be...
A Beautiful Sunflower Sol named Tunisia RaWanda.
A Creative Braid Floetic Sculptress Artist,
who's just getting started watering her garden.

This is a reminder to you...
That everything you do affects your hair too boo...
So Stay Trū. Be Yoū.™
Asé?

Asé.

— Tunisia RaWanda

Payne

I'm in a different energy today.
My mind be in a slight calamity.
Trying to make sense of what was forcibly handed to me.
When it comes to my ancestry.
More importantly our hair you see…

Now I get why they say laughter is good for the soul.
That's why I make sure I get my laughter, my giggle and my tickle on.
Then I rewind it back when I get a crack.

It all makes sense.
Taking me back to this series.
That I use to watch in the 90's reminding me…

Of it being funny how they would kick us out of every scene. Like how Martin would do Tommy, Cole and Pam.
Only to point and laugh at our beaded beads.

Until...
Two beautiful sisters came on the scene.
And punished everything.
With their beaded beads to the nation.
Now all of a sudden those points and laughs...
Turned into smiles and standing ovations.

That switch-up was diabolical.
That I felt those chills all through my hair follicles.
We ain't no fools we don't want your 40 acres and a mule.
We playing it cool by our own rules.

We up now, so get off our necks now.
Let's continue to pay attention,
to the prescriptions being given.
By reading the descriptions,
imprinted in the small indentions...

Of how our hair has been informing us,
of it being a glorified crown.
To them trying to tear it down because we woke now.

"Telegram telegram this is a high-value message..."
Coming to my window pane.
As I'm keen into the ivory weigh-ins.
We are significant.
Highly protected.

Wait...
What you mean there are laws explaining how our hair is distract-
ing...
Oh I get it.
You're probably mad even sad.
That your hair can't even grasp the same brush pad.

Nah it's deeper than that, you see...
Our hair are the antennas.
Connecting us to our higher beings.
That's why we be so deep in our feelings,
when we have a bad hair day…

(...you reading this...can you relate in any way?)

At any rate...
It's so much deeper to our variety hair show.
With your presence reading right now.
Close you eyes and imagine taking a look around.

You kinked up, I'm loc'd up, she braided up.
They whirly and sometimes we all want to catch that perfect spiral.
You know that's why our hair always goes viral.

When you look deep within, know our hair was never a sin.
So look again. And Ascend.
Just know the beauty of your innher flow shows in your hair
growth.

— Tunisia RaWanda

Enchanted Forest

Riding on the winds of enchantment
and the wings of dreams

In a world of mystical creatures
where fairy tales and nightmares meet

Anything is possible
as spellbinding transformations take hold

Myths and legends take root
in every grain of sand
and molecule in the air

Where the unexplainable and intangible
flow of life force roams free
Where reality gives way to fantasy
and fantasy becomes reality

To the truth of common knowledge
of which none applies here

There are no boundaries
and limitations are nonexistent

Moonlight caresses the oceans
as stars dance across the sky

The desire of thoughts are all granted
within a conscious mind

Planets and galaxies align perfectly
as the universe echoes tranquility

— Watson John

Just Try Jesus

Just try Jesus and he will never let you down.
Just try Jesus and he will never let you fall.
Just try Jesus, he will be there through it all.

Is what the song says—
people seem to try every solution
except the best solution.

The answer is Jesus.

Some people have the nerve to get angry
when other people suggest that Jesus is the best solution
for any problem.

Jesus is the rhyme and reason.
Jesus is the reason for the season.
Jesus is rhythm and blues.
Jesus is hip hop.

Jesus is anything
you can conceptualize in your mind
that is goodness, faithfulness, and honesty.

My solemn cry
to people doin' wrong:
just try Jesus.

— Poetic Messiah Willie James Lee, III

I want my poetry to...

I want my poetry to heal
to help the broken all survive their pain
to give them back the life they cannot feel
to show them that tomorrow's not in vain

I want my poetry to purge
the conscience of the seedy and their gain
ill-gotten with a sordid, selfish urge
and stop another heart from being slain

I want my poetry to move
a shattered heart to swim before it drowned
and lift it up the mountain that will prove
there's hope beyond their sorrow to be found

I want my poetry to save
to help the broken-hearted to forgive
to put them on the road that's past the grave
and piece together love so they can live

— Carthornia Kouroupos

The Words Aren't Gone

Empty pages
Still pens
Blank notes
Frozen QWERTY keys
The words…
Where have the words gone?

Countless days since the last writing
Haven't lost motivation
But inspiration has taken a leave of absence
It's the kind of betrayal that creatives wish
we didn't know so well
Forcing it amounts to lackluster results
Crumpled paper
Journals landing on the other side of the room
You feel like throwing your phone or laptop
But the last thing you need is to be both
wordless and device-less

The words aren't gone

Go for a walk and let nature take you to a
portal you never knew existed
Let the breeze blow you into a new corner of the world
Hug a tree and be taken to a peaceful, zen-like space
Recapture joy in an activity you love
but haven't done in a while
Go see that exhibit you've been meaning to checkout
at your favorite gallery or museum
Watch that movie with the scenes that keep replaying in your head—
there's probably a message lying there

The words aren't gone

Sometimes the routine needs to change
Sometimes new or familiar experiences can
jumpstart our creative engine
Sometimes life needs to teach us a few more things
before we can fill the pages again

The words aren't gone

While the worry and frustration is understandable—
It won't make you push through this period any faster
All creatives go through this
Give yourself grace, be patient, and try shaking things up
a little bit

The words aren't gone

Sometimes all we need is a little rejuvenation
And at some miraculous, magical moment shortly thereafter—
The words will flow again.

— Buddah Desmond

The Poet Messiah

Organically chosen, I am the savior for my cause
The revolution of poetry is here, and to me, that torch falls

I am not bound by a four-cornered room,
I stand here with no walls
In the open, where what you see is what you get:
the good, the bad, and all the flaws

The creativity of your artistry is your own;
there are no correct procedures or regulatory laws
No one must be a sacrificial lamb,
so there's no reason to draw straws

It may not always prove a simple task,
negotiating the affections of life's vicious claws
Self-motivation is required,
for there may not always be an approving outward applause

Fear not for he is here—The Poet Messiah
I have come to enlighten your minds and take you higher
Representing the possibilities of your deepest desire

There are numerous ways to navigate
thru the perplexity of this paralyzing paradox

Keep the inherent trait of adaptability
like that of the clever fox

Be mentally and physically strong
like that of the massive ox

Keep your mind as free as the wind
remaining outside of that box

Stand up for what you believe in,
not hiding your hand if you throw the rocks

Be hardy with expectation,
remaining ready when opportunity knocks

Position oneself to obtain every key to all the locks
Stay diligently consistent with the time set on all life's clocks

Suffering along the way
with the awareness of potholes and roadblocks

Fear not for he is here—The Poet Messiah
I have come to enlighten your minds and take you higher
Representing the possibilities of your deepest desire

A meticulous work ethic is what will speak for me
As I remain steadfast thru the storms of life,
grounded and rooted like that of a Giant Sequoia tree

These storms can be savagely unpredictable
like those of the Bering Sea

Finding comfort in knowing
that the sun will rise to brighten the horizon is the key

It takes time to reach that next level,
a far deeper degree

The Poet Messiah—he is I and I am he

— Watson John

Chapter 6:
The Final Chorus

Closing voices of power, resilience, collective unity.

In the end, the voices gather. Gratitude and grief, defiance and hope, blend into one last sound — a chorus that carries forward the collective strength of the pen beyond the page, refusing silence.

Sunday Serenade

My tears fall
like prayers I did not mean to say,
unfolding without shame
or apology,
sliding down the skin
of this weathered body—
a map of ache
etched in salt and silence.

My chest is a hollowed-out chapel
where hymns used to live.
now, only echoes.
now, only breath
trying to remember how to stay.

The salt stings as my eyes
flutter open—
half in dream,
half in dread—
to greet another day
I never asked for,
wrapped in light
I don't yet know how to hold.

Grief curls beneath my ribs
like smoke from a fire
that never truly went out—
just smoldered,
quiet and cunning,
waiting for the stillness
to rise again.

My limbs are exhausted —
not just from lack of sleep,
but from surviving
what I cannot name aloud.

Even the sheets feel too heavy,
woven with yesterdays
that still will not let me go.

But....

morning light
slips in anyway—
soft, stubborn,
like grace that forgot
I stopped believing.

And outside,
a sparrow sings
her Sunday serenade,
notes stitched with morning
and mercy,
as if she has been waiting
just for me.

Her song cuts clean
through the hush—
not loud,
but sure.
as if to say:

you are still here.
you are still here.

And somehow,
that is enough.
not because the pain has passed,
but because I dared
to open my eyes again.
to breathe,
to weep,
to listen.

And maybe—
just maybe—
that little bird
was always meant
to find me.

— Amy Michelle Kennedy

Grateful and Blessed

When I think about how I live,
I thank God for giving me a mind to strive—
and that's no jive.

For He supplies all my needs,
and a path for this chick to succeed,
to collect all those proceeds.

Which enables me to make a lot of cash,
so this chick can talk so much trash.

Now here I stand before you in a flash;
so there will be no need for us to clash.

While I continue to collect and
hide all that stash—
which will allow me to forget about my past
and to end this fast.

For writing this was a blast.

— Cassandra Reed-Anderson

Waiting for the Sun

Tree branches lean low
Brace against the angry wind
Waiting for the sun

— Carthornia Kouroupos

City Streets

Leaves blow from branches
Crawl roughly across asphalt
Colorful explosion

— Carthornia Kouroupos

Homeless

Walls seemed to close in on me last night,
so cold and lonely as I stared at the streetlight.
Laid in a cardboard box, I called my bed—
hard being homeless, hopeless, and unfed.

Hoped that sleep came quickly so reality fades;
dreamt of a better future as I quietly laid.

Homelessness is not a sin, curse, or crime—
a matter of position in my life, at this given time.
Lived on the street, I am not sick in my head.
Finance took me down, job and home got shred.

My faith is tested; when all hope seems to be gone,
sometimes hard to focus ahead, hard to move on.

Being homeless for a year, tried to survive;
in and around the streets, I stayed alive.
My God is able and stands by me each day;
He laid His hand on me and took my pain and shame away.

Now at the shelter, being fed and possibly not homeless,
confident in God for a better tomorrow that He promises.

— Sandra Dawn Swaby Robinson

Live Your Best Life

I carry with me the scars of mental illness.
Like a thermostat is cast,
I've had multiple episodes of highs and lows,
swept up by desires of longings
and willingness to change.

Have escaped my plateau
and found serenity in the midst of
chaos, confusion, unseen dangers, and bouts of rows.

Things seemed chaotic all around.
Like congregants in confession,
I took everything that's silly—as worth confessing,
often acting more like a comical clown.
Thought I was winning, though acting "willy-nilly."

I didn't think I was so confused.
I'd led a life of a work-a-lick.
What could it be that sparked the fuse?
Everything tasted and felt more like colic,
and caused me to be in a feeling of melancholy.

They say "it's an ill-wind that blows no good."
I've had to do lots of soul searching.
Of everything I'd shun,
took thinking into overdrive—
of what I thought I should.
Met thoughts with triumph and disaster,
although the journey had just begun.

I threw temper tantrums,
as I literally lashed out too.
Thought my thoughts were worth caressing,
but were simply not a blessing.

195

I was a nervous, nerdy wreck.
No one wanted to be a part of
my conjured-up confusing crew.

I had to find my magic markers—
put pen, pencil, crayon, and
whatever writing tools at hand's grasp,
to come out of the doldrums of despair.

With hands held clasp,
I spoke words into existence to the Deity,
then transported them to paper,
in my willingness, my experiences to share—
sometimes, though not life at its best.

I began a hopeful remedy,
seeking help from those around—even the shrinks.
Thoughts though seemed futile.
I took up singing as a melody,
but was chastised and pointed out to me:
my blissful singing was wild.

There were times when I didn't consult the Divine,
and got into unseen dangers
that ripped me mercilessly apart.
Meandering down the streets of my mind,
I did and said things I later regretted.

Like an attacking lion or shark,
I had to be heavily medicated.
Long from the road of a wounded lark,
I've emerged as I have been educated
to what's acclaimed as acceptable behavior—
and more in that of acceptance,
and not the wounds of my Savior.

My Bible I've learned to quietly read.
The pages contained writings
that were like heaven-sent,
though some of its content I often dreaded—
brought with its plenty consolation
to my heart's content.

I've come a long way from insanity,
from the crude past of inconsistency.
Accepting that I had a disease or disability
was by reason the quickest way
to solve the mystery.

Looking back, I saw I was living
a life on the fast track.
Like a ship on the ocean is tossed,
I faced dangerous dilemma
of finding my true identity.

I had to choose quickly,
as I looked at my life in flashback—
whether I'd rather keep repeatedly erroneous deeds
or match my truth like a religious creed.

I've come a mighty long way.
My mindset manages my heartfelt emotions,
my thoughtful thinking, my valiant values and actions.
I've meandered many critics whose words
made me feel like an obnoxious outcast
and may have pushed me into notions of negativity
that caused a chain reaction.

But I've made a promise to my meticulous mind
to live my best life—
my redemption to cast.

I'm now living my best life.
Though faced with challenges in multiple forms,
I'm learning daily to best shun upheaval and strife.
I sometimes have to go against norms
to elevate self, to bring depth to my soul.

Like iron in a process is mold,
I am a work of art to behold.

"Live your best life" is more than a cliché.
Thoughts conjured up, actions to prove,
deeds to the rescue—
talents to hone and craft,
hearts to woo and longings to fulfill.

Life's not just a dream in draft,
but acts done and skills to learn and grow,
to meet a life that's more than a thrill.

I've developed the art and craft of my hobbies—
singing, dancing, listening to music,
even expression of self in journals.

Wherever I go, even in lobbies,
meeting and making new friendships
in settings formal or informal.

Being true to my passions
has seen scales fall from mine eyes.
But staying true to my actions,
acknowledging that what I have is enough,
was what I needed—even if they mayn't be everything
to cover up my stuff.

Stand tall, let no man treat you like a moron.
Thoughts to the road to recovery—a long haul.
Though long and winding and at times consuming,
find solace and pleasure in simplicity.

Fill self with gratitude graciously,
and not one spent in regrets, bouts of bawl,
or a life of uttering profanity.

Put your faith in God to the test.
Be as cool as cucumber
when the pressures of life are paramount.
Dancing in the rain and not complaining
will bring you a life lived at its truest—best.

— Claudette R. Cox

It's About To Be On!

It's about to be on!
Sweet potato pone
or pie.

Coconut, apple, cherry are more than enough
to make a dessert fork cry—

because it has to choose
between 7-Up, lemon, apple jelly,
sour cream/cream cheese pound or triple layer cake,
yet it can't lose.

Those sweets have roll call at the kitchen table.
Diets are not able
to stand firm
against this culinary assault,
as eyes begin to water and fingertips squirm.

Peach and blackberry cobbler stand in the corner,
beckoning your palate,
since they have been waiting all year
for this day of reckoning.

Cornish hens
believe it's a sin
to be placed next to beef.
The dining room looks at all of this cooking in disbelief.

Ham hocks and neck bones stand tall,
while collards, turnips, and mustards have a ball—
sitting with their legs crossed in steam,
sipping on a pot liquor's dream.

The chitlins attempt to tease only angers rice.
In frustration, hot sauce shouts out to the crowd,
"We all have to get along, so play nice!"

Hog maws pull pig tails;
in outrage pig ears wail.
Fatback high fives okra and black-eyed peas.
Chicken flirts with oil as it begins to weaken
and falls to its knees.

Cornmeal's mind wanders,
and the cast iron skillet yells at it to pay attention.
Turkey wings simmer on the stove,
complaining about their pension.

Flour gets caught making gravy.
The oven proudly announces,
"I am going to have a baby!"

Macaroni and cheese
sassily tells the pan that she aims to please.

Dressing and stuffing
tussle hard for a few minutes,
then go back to their corners huffing and puffing.

Celery, eggs, and mayonnaise
have a wrestling match in a bowl.
Salt and pepper strut into the room
because they have soul.

Once dried,
limas, navy, and pinto beans
swell with pride
as the crock pot comes on the scene.

Buttermilk and shortening elope.
Spatula hugs the grill
and tells it not to give up on hope.

Lemons try to ambush pineapples,
so coffee runs to get Kool-Aid and tea.

Cream of tartar happily plans a caper
with bananas and vanilla wafers.

Timer, unconcerned with its survival,
hollers at apron about my pending arrival.

I step into the kitchen and to my delight—
all is calm and bright.

— Colette D. Jones

The Cricket

Woven from an imagination that never fails,
this fairy tale
holds the buried fancies of a little girl turned woman—
summoned
by loneliness and what she thinks is lack.

Strolling toward a pond, she lies on her back,
pondering,
wondering
if she would ever find love.

A wicked sign that was rejected from up above
bounces to her in the form of a cricket.
It hops out of a thicket,
making a noise
that makes her press pause
on her thoughts.

Caught
up in his unusual melody,
she leans over to get a better look as a less-than-heavenly
light shines, and immediately she is amazed—
fully dazed.

Her eyes develop an unnatural sheen.
He starts to preen,
his wings
fluttering evilly, he continues to sing,
conjuring visions of the perfect man—
one she hastily thinks does more than just understand
her needs.

As her mind begins to bleed,
foolishly opening her heart,
the line
intertwined
with her spirit and psyche drift apart.

The cricket chants
an ancient spell as he performs a malevolent dance,
making her subconscious spasm.
He permanently deepens the chasm
between reality and perception,
completing his immoral conception.

He transforms into his sinful shape,
grabbing her by the nape,
catching her totally unaware,
realizing too late that her soul was screaming beware.

Now frozen with horrified shock,
her essence hellishly locked,
she looks up and sees her wish was a nightmare in disguise.

Unfortunately, her impatience became her demise,
for she will have eternity to consider when to rein in her feelings
that ran amok,
or who told her that crickets meant good luck.

— Colette D. Jones

De la Gaia

Daybreak,
Jaguar Butterfly hovered,
syringed the velvety watermelon,
jetted.

Around noon,
Cheetah Monarch marked the black-eyed Susans.
Her dust-strewn pollen trail—
yellow, pungent, sticky.

Wren chased Cheetah Monarch,
tweezed black-eyed Susan,
pecked her, tossed his head, then
jetted.

Evening Star's white glow
melted the dark,
turned the shimmery green, rose-gold,
the lawn black and cool.

Before dawn,
Dew dropped clear beads on grass tips.
Cheetah and Leopard jet-streamed
through purple-blue abundance.

— E N Dalili

Savanna Blues

The cool stone against my neck, I cuddle stone,
earth, hardened brick.
Necking my stone-walled lover cools me.

No heat—
passion flat against my cheek,
disregard the long-leafed trees.

I nuzzle the stony barrier,
memories of my breezy savanna,
flexing thoughts of home—of her.

Our sunset dance,
prancing,
our one-two-three step romance.

Black birds marked time while we danced,
necks entwined.
I blink the memory, then

cooled again by the stony wall,
its rough surface
reminds me:
to survive is to stumble through closed-lid dreams.

I scratch her itchy,
cold, stone head,
bumpy surface and all.
I neck the wall.

— E N Dalili

Bullets in the Fire

Prophet or pariah,
I threw bullets into fire—
only to cement my desire
to commit my soul to aspire.

By committing this feverous deed,
I succumbed to my selfish-foolish needs
that would not heed.

Yet, I did not yield
to Mother Nature's speed.
That one's life purpose
must be righteous and true
for their soul to reap.

— Edward Roy

They

She doesn't want me to see you
because he doesn't want me to see you
because she's afraid I might fall in love
and he's afraid I might leave home,
but no one's asked me anything.

She doesn't want me to kiss you
because he doesn't want me to kiss you
because she's afraid a kiss might lead to something else
and he's afraid because he knows a kiss will lead to something
else,
but no one's asked me anything.

She doesn't want to hear me talk about you
because he doesn't want to hear me talk about you
because she's afraid I might start talking about marriage
and he's afraid I'm growing up,
but no one's asked me anything.

She would rather see us apart
because he would rather see us apart
because she's afraid to see me grow up
and he's afraid I already have,
but no one's asked me anything.

— Graemme Denyce Boone

Monster In The Closet

I sit with fire in my throat
A steady thud in my chest.
War drums and war cries, not warnings.
I want to set flames to everything
that ever thought it could
snuff me out and walk away unscathed.

I feel my teeth crack
under the pressure of restraint.
Lockjaw from years
of locking away what should've been screams.
My nails curl like claws,
digging trenches into my palms
until blood flows like oceans
fed by my own fury.

I sit stone-faced, eyes fixed
not on an escape
but on the most strategic point of attack.
The nearest exit?
Not for my safety.
It's where I'll be standing,
blocking yours.

One wrong word.
One careless step.
And I'll let the rage level everything
it can touch.
Years of silence,
every damn time I bit my tongue
until it bled in my mouth,
now turned to fuel.

The demon I tucked away
in a closet with prayer and therapy
she's stirring.
She stretches her neck,
cracks her knuckles,
grins with all her sharp teeth.

"Let me out", she purrs.
"just for tonight."

Her fingers curl beneath the doorframe,
tapping out Morse Code,
only I know how to read.
She whispers in my ear
like a lover turned executioner
"Let it Burn"

I clench harder
Dig deeper
Taste Iron
Taste fury
Pain grounds me
and rage flicks the match

"Please?", she asks again
this time sweet, saccharine
and my mouth curls.
Not in kindness.
In memory.
That crooked smirk
I once feared in the mirror
now mirrors hers.

Like a shark in water,
I smell blood
my own
but I do not flinch
I bite
and open her door.

She steps out,
Grabs a cigarette like a trophy,
and towers over me
Like the shadow, I tried to starve
She hugs me
tight
Like I'm hers again.

"Ready?" she asks.
I nod.

She gathers every insult,
every dismissal,
every time I was overlooked or underestimated
and alchemizes it into gasoline.

We start in the corners.
then the heart of the room.
She douses it all.

"See?" She states matter-of-factly.
"They never loved you like I do."

She leads me to the door,
takes one last drag
and flicks the cigarette over her shoulder.

The room erupts,
an altar for the girl who stayed silent.

She lights another
smirks at me
"You need me."

I take her cigarette
Breathe her in
Feel her fire become mine
and we say together,
"I always have."

— Sh'Quelle Brown

QUIET!

They told us
be quiet.
Not in screams,
but in sharp glances,
tight smiles,
and 50 cent raises for how well we played small.
They told us
Be polite,
like shrinking brought peace.
Like softness was our salvation.
Like we were still paying the price
over a bitten apple.
They told us
be seen, not heard,
unless we were humming lullabies,
Stroking their... ego.
or plating their dinner.
They told us-
Don't be *too* loud.
Don't be *too* direct.
Don't be *too* passionate.
Don't be *too* angry.
They told us,
Be a girl, not a *problem*.
Watch your attitude.
That your "No!" actually means
"playing hard to get"
They told us,
You're Dismissed.
You're underqualified.
You're *too* emotional.
They told us,
Our rage was criminal
Our power, stake-able.

Our womanhood, political.
They told us
You need to apologize
for feeling
for not measuring our dresses
for not being grateful to be rebranded
by a cheap ring on our left finger.
But silence was never safety.
Silence was a burial.
And we've been exhuming ourselves
line by line,
truth by truth,
scream by scream.
Generation after generation.
So NO!
Do not be quiet!
Not now.
Not then.
Not ever again.
Do not dim your voice
to make their comfort more
comfortable.
Do not whisper your stories
so they can sleep soundly
on systems built on our silence,
threaded by an idea that we
came from a rib.
Do not forget that we bring life
not the other way around.
Do not forget that this voice,
your voice
IS the system.

— Sh'Quelle Brown

Something Within

Like the seasons, there is a time
for the birth of newness, the shedding of what was,
so that something valuable, secretly hidden from view
no longer wrestles tireless to be free.
There is such a time.

If the one held captive should know the exact moment,
would that one hasten towards the offering of peace?
Or would we hear squeaking and squawking,
"Not yet, not now, not me!"
(Clinging to yesterday, going nowhere faster and faster.)

So then, when is this time?
This ideal place or space—the right season
to burst forth strong and joyously—fragrant
in the embrace of The Beautiful Divine.

In the fullness of time,
answer the call.

— Mildred M. Stokes

No Division in Heaven

On Sunday morning down here,
we divide.
Some sway to gospel choirs,
hands lifted high in a Black church,
where the organ runs like thunder,
and every "Amen" feels like fire.

Others sit in white pews,
hymnals open,
voices neat and measured,
a white church polished with silence,
every prayer whispered,
every nod restrained.

Catholics kneel,
lighting candles for the saints.
Baptists plunge you
beneath the waters of the river.
Pentecostals speak in tongues,
dancing barefoot in the Spirit.
But Church of God in Christ—
they wouldn't dare,
for what one calls holy
another calls strange,
and what one calls worship
another calls wrong.

Down here,
we draw our lines with doctrine,
with dress codes,
with "we do this"
and "they don't do that."

But up there—
in the wide arms of eternity,
there is no Black church,
no white church,
no Catholic,
no Baptist,
no Pentecostal robe or crown.

No division in heaven.
Only voices blending—
a choir of every nation,
every tongue,
singing not against each other
but with each other.

And the only robe that matters
is the one of light,
woven by grace.

— Noah Rivers

11:59 pm

In the future
>We are happy
>We are equal
>We are free

In the future
>We choose who we want to be
>Read banned books
>Participate in peaceful protests without the threat of incar-
>ceration deportation termination

In the future
>No person is above the law
>Taking a knee becomes the Sixth Freedoms of the First
>Amendment
>Pro-slavery anthem better known as the Star-Spangled
>Banner is stricken from history

In the future
Tick
In the future
Tick
In the future

— Nicole Lanier Montez

Death

Death is so hard to face—
a time when emotions go bending out of shape,
trying to understand and accept why
Your loved one had to die.

When death comes your way,
ask God for more strength each day.
Death brings you deep sorrow;
Strong faith in God brings a brighter tomorrow.

Life is short, live it right.
Wasted energy to argue, fuss, and fight.
Make the most of your lives together.
When death intervenes, only memories last forever.

Expression of love you rarely show—
When they're loved, let them know.
You have today to get it right.
Tomorrow doesn't guarantee your life.

Live life to its fullest every day.
Express your love in every possible way.
Let God be the center of your lives.
When death arrives, through Him you'll survive.

— Sandra Dawn Swaby Robinson

Negativity

Negative thoughts consume your brain,
blood pulsing viciously in your vein.
Why do you allow this emotion to take control—
acting out of character, being cold.

Negative behavior, violent action,
taking life's frustration out on another man.
Screaming, yelling, words of abuse;
destruction of the body with smoking, drugs, and booze.

Negative friends only keep you down.
In times of trouble, they are never around.
Keep friends who guide, positively help you to aim high,
and will rejoice with you, as you reach for the sky.

Negative future, no goals set out for you—
wondering through life aimlessly in this society too.
Blaming the world for your lack of responsibility,
for not climbing the ladder of success and all its possibilities.

Turn negativity into possibility.
Life is too short, live it wisely.
Face life challenges with God as your guide,
and negativity for sure will fall along the wayside.

— Sandra Dawn Swaby Robinson

Rubber Band Man

Rubber Band Man, yeah he snaps back.
He doesn't care about anybody else's feelings,
'cause his emotions are so out of whack.

Rubber band man will do anything to survive—
from cocaine to heroin sells,
to nicks and dime bags of weed just to get by
and try to get a piece of the pie.

Rubber band man never realized
that it was only two ways out of his lifestyle:
the jail cell or untimely demise.

So one day Rubber Band Man was pressed for time.
He tried to stretch out for one last time.
Unfortunately he snapped—
never to snap back again.

— Poetic Messiah Willie James Lee, III

221

Who Are You?
Spoken Word Edition

Who am I? Let me set it straight,
A woman of power, I carry my weight.
Resources deep, resilience strong,
Tenacity drives me to keep moving along.
When I'm in my zone, let me create,
Don't interrupt—just let me relate.
I see the pieces, how they align,
Inner-standing the picture takes its time.
Thoughts come rushing, uninvited they stay,
But I'm the landlord—I choose who pays.
I'm thanksgiving woman, gratitude in my hand,
Passionate fire, a voice that commands.
Yes, I talk loud, yes, I talk fast,
But my extra is gold, built to last.
I'm the door monitor, check that wristband,
No ticket, no entry—you'll understand.
I'm the wedding coordinator, bold and true,
"Family, it's not your day—this ain't about you."
I'm physical touch, so don't neglect,
Brushes and hugs, that's how I connect.
I need conversation, consistency too,
I pour into you—so pour back, boo.
I'm about meaning, no small talk play,
Knowledge exchanged in a soulful way.
Kinesthetic learner, I must do to believe,
Words hit deeper when my hands achieve.
I'm a "man's word is his bond" type queen,
So speak it real, keep your promise clean.
I've got a comedic side, sarcastic wit,
Ask me a question, you might get a skit.
A grunt, a smirk, or a sound that's sly,
Wisdom wrapped in humor, sharp as the eye.
I'm observant, watchful, guarding my space,

Life taught me boundaries, I know my place.
I'll tell you quick when you're crossing the line,
Protecting my peace, protecting what's mine.
I am you, and you are me,
Reflections mirrored, soul set free.
Melanated, real, flaws and grace,
Hang ups, hiccups—I still embrace.
B cups, but big spirit, can't box me in,
Every struggle I faced just sharpened my grin.
I rise, I fall, I love, I laugh,
I carve my story, I own my path.
So who am I? The answer is clear,

A woman of presence—remember me here.

— Q Denise Masten

Joy Is a Drumbeat

Joy is a drumbeat
that no chain can silence,
a rhythm stitched into the soles of our feet,
calling us to rise,
to move,
to breathe in color.

We dance because the body remembers
what the mind forgets—
that freedom is not a theory,
it is hips swaying,
hands clapping,
laughter spilling into the air like brass horns.

Every note a rebellion,
every step a survival story
told without words.

The music finds us,
even in the darkest corners,
and when it does,
we do not ask permission—
we lift our voices,
lift our bodies,
lift each other,

until the sound itself
is enough to split the night open
and flood it with light.

— Genesis Lyric

The Sound of the Collective Pen

Closing Poem

It does not end here.
The book may close,
but the voices keep moving—
through pulp and ink,
through memory and mouth,
through every ear willing to listen.

We heard the whispers of *Love*,
the laments of *Loss*.
We walked through *Faith* and *Fire*,
found *Healing* in the shadows,
and carried *Hope* like a banner into tomorrow.

Together, these chapters
form more than a book.
They form a map of the human heart—
its fractures,
its resilience,
its endless will to keep beating.

And so the sound of the collective pen
does not belong to the poets alone.
It belongs to every reader
who dares to carry these words forward,
to answer ink with ink,
to remember and to respond.

Because the words are not gone.
The words live on.
And the sound of the collective pen
is still being written—
in you.

— Aaron C. Butler

About the Contributors

A.W Jackson

An award-winning author, poet, and writer originally from Waldorf, Maryland, and now based in North Carolina, Jackson's passion for poetry began in high school and has grown into more than a decade of dedicated writing. The author of two published poetry collections, he seeks to provide readers with tools for self-discovery and resilience. Through his work, he aims to inspire others to believe in themselves and persevere in the face of life's challenges. A.W.'s poems in this anthology include *County Fair*, *Jordan River*, and *Harmony Retreat*.

Amy Michelle Kennedy

A published poet and author, Kennedy's work reflects themes of grief, healing, and resilience. Her three poetry collections—*Where the Wildflowers Grow*, *Sacred from the Shattered*, and *Every Scar, Every Light*—invite readers into an honest exploration of loss and hope, offering words that both console and inspire. Through her writing, she seeks to honor the human spirit and the transformative power of poetry. Amy's poems in this anthology include *The Mirror They Threw*, *Blueprint of My Sky*, and *Sunday Serenade*.

Andrew Kouroupos

A writer whose work has been featured in several anthologies, Kouroupos also had his screenplay *Homeboys* showcased at the Sundance Film Festival, highlighting his versatility across genres. Most recently, his short story *Odee* was nationally recognized as one of the top 50 short stories of 2024 by Josephson Entertainment and Roadmap Writers. He continues to explore storytelling in multiple forms, bringing depth and originality to each project. Andrew's poems in this anthology include *Boy Blue*, *Rebel Son*, and *Dead Poets Society*.

Annie C. Maclin-Johnson

An award-winning author, member of the Phi Theta Kappa Honor Society, and former realtor, Maclin-Johnson found great joy in helping families achieve the dream of homeownership. Her lifelong goal, however, was to become a published author—a dream she realized in August 2023 with the release of her first book, *WHO SAID THAT?*, which won the LitStar Book Award for Outstanding Children's Book. She has since launched a growing series that encourages children to develop a positive mindset toward their physical features, skin tone, and hair. Through titles such as *WHO DID THAT?* and *FOUR EYES ADVANTAGE?*, she shows that even young children can make a meaningful difference in society. In *WHO IS THAT?*, Maclin-Johnson invites children to embrace the wisdom and love of grandparents, celebrating the legacy of family history. Annie's poems in this anthology include *In My Skin*, *What About My Nose and Mouth?*, and *Four Eyes Advantage*.

Aryianna "Ari" Edmond

A youth contributor to this anthology, Ari brings an exuberant voice and a natural gift for communication. Speaking in full sentences by the age of one, she quickly earned the nickname "Talk-A-Lot" from her teachers and has often been recognized with class awards such as "Future Politician," "Future Activist," and "Class Public Speaker." Passionate about many forms of art, she brings big ideas to life through poetry, using her words to explore equality, respect, and imagination. Even at just nine years old, Ari is a vocal advocate for fairness and kindness, often gathering her family to share her latest work. As a big sister, she hopes to inspire her younger siblings with the magic of poetry, demonstrating that creativity is a powerful force present in every act of creation. Aryianna's poems in this anthology include *My ARTerial Vein*, *Man's Best Friend*, and *Breaking Generational Curses*.

Buddah Desmond (BDez)

A poet, writer, artist, singer, entrepreneur, health and wellness advocate, and UX professional based in the DMV, Desmond's work draws from lessons of adversity and triumph, offering messages of hope, love, healing, and resilience. They are the author of six poetry collections, including *Prevail: Poems on Life, Love, and Politics* (2012), *From the Inside Out: A Poetry Collection* (2020), and *Coming Up From the Downside: Finding Joy in Our Song* (2024). Their writing has been featured in numerous publications such as *Creative Currents*, *Rebel's Zeitgeist*, *Liquid Cat Quarterly*, and *MUSED*. Desmond has also served as a healing leader with The Sanctuaries (DC) and currently serves on the National Board of Trustees of Gamma Xi Phi, the professional arts fraternity. Buddah's poems in this anthology include *NOUNS*, *Two-Stepping Between Power + Evil*, and *The Words Aren't Gone*.

Carthornia Kouroupos

A professor at Rowan College of South Jersey, Kouroupos teaches English, Oral Communication, and African American Literature. She holds an M.A. in Writing Arts from Rowan University and has contributed to several publications, including *The 26th Annual Poetry Ink*, *The Year of the Poet IX*, *The Year of the Poet X*, and *Letter Poems to Our Deceased*. Her poetry collection *Filling Gaps with Broken Pieces* was published by Inner Child Press. Kouroupos is also the author of several children's books, including *Zoe the Clam*, *Zoe the Clam Goes to School*, *Denny and the Wizard: It's a Fairytale*, and *Another Alexander*. Through her poetry and storytelling, she seeks to inspire readers of all ages to become the best versions of themselves. Carthornia's poems in this anthology include *I want my poetry to…*, *Waiting for the Sun*, and *City Streets*.

Cassandra Reed-Anderson

Born and raised in Washington, D.C., Reed-Anderson is a proud graduate of Ballou High School and Strayer University. She is the mother of two children, Aaron and LaKeyetta, and the grandmother of Nalani, Leila, and Marco. Her love of words has led her to publish

229

her first poems, marking an important milestone in her creative journey. She writes with gratitude, faith, and pride, drawing inspiration from her family and community. Cassandra's poems in this anthology include *Black Is Me* and *Grateful and Blessed*.

Claudette R. Cox

A poet and early childhood education teacher, Cox's love for language and learning shines through her work. She is the author of two poetry collections, *Love Knows No Boundaries* and *A Closer View*, available on Amazon and Kindle. Born in St. Mary, Jamaica, to parents Roland and Myrtle Cox, she is one of ten siblings and the proud mother of her daughter, Andrean. Through her writing, Cox seeks to share perspectives of love, resilience, and humanity that transcend boundaries. Claudette's poem in this anthology is *Live Your Best Life*.

Colette D. Jones

A native of Columbia, South Carolina, and a retired Air Force veteran, Jones has traveled extensively across the world, boldly and unashamedly sharing her unfathomable love of poetry. As an "artivist" for over 30 years, she has used poetry both to minister and to address social issues plaguing communities and the world. Jones embraces the power of words with dignity and care. She writes for healing, inspiration, and empowerment, while pushing through negativity or poison until the ink of her mind, heart, and spirit is clear. Colette's poems in this anthology include *My People*, *It's About To Be On!*, and *The Cricket*.

Edward Roy

Author of *Bullets in the Fire: The Biography of New York Red* and *The Ugly Secrets of Private Roy*, Roy was born in Atlanta, Georgia, to Erma L. Hill and raised in Harlem under her determined guidance, which helped him resist the pull of the streets. Mentored by Malcolm X and others, he graduated high school, served in the U.S. Army's Medical Corps, and later completed college with the support of his mother's entrepreneurial spirit. After a successful career in corporate America, he turned to writing to share his remarkable life story. Edward's poem in this anthology is *Bullets in the Fire*.

E N Dalili

Dalili performs poetry in Baltimore and leads a virtual poetry workshop for writers living in Oakland, Germany, Baltimore, and Washington, D.C. She performed a water ceremony for the memorial dedication to the enslaved Africans of John McDonogh and an original spoken word piece for the Human Trafficking exhibit at the Watergate Gallery. Her poetry has appeared in the *Beltway Journal*, and her chapbook *Ra Anx Heh* explores themes of heritage and spirituality. She is currently working on a collection of poetry on the authority of nature. Dalili's poems in this anthology include *De la Gaia* and *Savanna Blues*.

Genesis Lyric

At just seventeen, Lyric is a rising poet from the United Kingdom whose voice carries the cadence of the London spoken word scene. Rooted in rhythm and performance, her work bridges page and stage, drawing inspiration from music, community, and the power of language to move people. She writes about beginnings, resilience, and joy, infusing her lines with both lyrical flow and emotional depth. Genesis's poems in this anthology include *Breath As Origin* and *Joy Is a Drumbeat*.

Graemme Denyce Boone

A Christian mother of six adult children and grandmother of fourteen, Boone has always had a passion for writing poetry and prose. She is the author of two memoirs, *Life: From Traumatic to Triumphant* and *Traveling the United States of America From the Atlantic Ocean to the Pacific Ocean: A Travel Memoir*, with a third currently in progress. Through her work, she seeks to encourage others to read and to believe that they can achieve anything they set their minds to. Despite many hardships and challenges, she has never stopped dreaming or creating. Her words inspire others to live their best life with courage and determination. Graemme's poems in this anthology include *Parents*, *Thank YOU, GOD!*, and *They*.

Itta-ZaVoni Rayelle Galmore (IZR Galmore)

An author whose work draws deeply from her personal life experiences, Galmore is a 2004 graduate of Beacon College who has faced significant health and mental health challenges, including a serious infection that required emergency surgery and a diagnosis of paranoid schizophrenia. Her first book, *Brainstorm* (2015), recounts her journey with mental health and the vital support of her family and community. Her most recent memoir, *Itta's Abscess in Her Left Breast: God Always Heals* (Christian Faith Publishing, 2023), documents her recovery from a life-threatening infection and the faith that sustained her. Galmore continues to find joy in writing poetry and stories that testify to resilience, faith, and the power of perseverance. Itta's poems in this anthology include *Hannah Faye's Faith*, *Magnolia*, and *Odesscia's...Song*.

Jada Ware

An emerging poet from Prince George's County, Maryland, Ware began writing at the age of twelve. For her, poetry and storytelling are not only ways to bring imagination to life but also pathways to deeper self-understanding and connection with others. Through the written word, she reflects on personal growth and explores how people connect across different perspectives. Ware views poetry as not only a form of expression but also a vehicle for connection and shared humanity. Jada's poem in this anthology is *Midnight Crown*.

Kaamilah Diabaté

A 25-year-old poet, Diabaté has been writing for more than a decade. Her most recognized piece, *X*, reflects the depth and honesty of her voice. Her poetry often explores the experience of growing up as a young Black woman and the journey of learning to embrace that identity. Through her work, she seeks to capture both the challenges and the beauty of self-discovery. Kaamilah's poems in this anthology include *Diary of a Broken Dream*, *X*, and *The Renegade*.

Ky'Lee Jamal

A writer dedicated to finding new ways to express himself through creative exploration, Jamal seeks opportunities to grow as an artist, bringing authenticity and real-life expression to every endeavor. Through his work, he channels experience into art, using poetry as a space to share truth and creativity with others. Ky'Lee's poem in this anthology is *Me*.

Leroy Negus McDowell Jr.

McDowell has been in love with words for as long as he can remember. He wrote his first poem in the 3rd grade and his first book in the 5th, a story that won his school's write-a-book contest and went on to compete at the county level. In middle school, a summer camp at the University of Maryland sparked his true passion for poetry, and soon after, he saw his byline in the *Prince George's Post* with front-page articles as a young intern. By high school, he was leading the journalism club and editing the school paper, then carried that love for writing into college, where he became editor and lead writer of the engineering club's magazine. Today, after three decades of writing—spanning poetry, journalism, and professional analysis—he has authored more than a hundred published works, some featured nationally, yet he still writes with the same wonder that began with a poem in a classroom notebook. Leroy's poems in this anthology include *Without Love, Love's Idea*, and *A Plea for Peace and Forgiveness*.

Linda Crosby

A U.S. Army veteran, published poet, and proud country girl, Crosby now resides in the South with her husband, Roy, and their beloved furbaby, Bella. A lover of music, religious programs, and classic cinema, she also enjoys reading biographies of Hollywood legends. Known to many as a "prayer warrior," she draws strength from her faith and the support of her family. Linda's poems in this anthology include *My Keeper, Give Yourself Consent*, and *More Skin In The Game*.

Lisa Nicole Kennedy

Writing since the age of twelve, Kennedy has cultivated a lifelong passion for storytelling. Her work often blends themes of fantasy, love, and nature, drawing readers into worlds both imagined and real. While some of her writing is inspired by lived experiences, she also delights in creating entirely new realms born from imagination and creativity. Lisa's poems in this anthology include *Guided by Light*, *Corner of Everlasting*, and *Raven's Cry*.

Mari the Poet

Writing with raw honesty about mental health, family, faith, and resilience, Mari's poetry offers both vulnerability and strength, confronting pain and transforming it into testimony. Through her work, she blends personal struggle with spiritual hope, giving voice to experiences that are often left unspoken. Her voice speaks to survival and the power of faith to heal and sustain. Mari's poems in this anthology include *if this is the last time i write a poem*, *Use Me Lord*, and *i love you*.

Marie Temple

Temple has faced the trials of addiction, domestic violence, abandonment, and feelings of worthlessness, yet found healing through poetry. Writing became her avenue to give voice to her pain and to discover peace and intimacy with God. Through her work, she invites readers to join her on a journey toward freedom and joy. Her poetry encourages others to release the burdens that bind them and embrace hope. Temple's debut poetry collection, *Life After Pain: The Journey of Getting There*, is available through Amazon, eBay, AuthorHouse, and Barnes & Noble. Marie's poems in this anthology include *I Do Not Cry*, *Snowflakes in the Dark*, and *The Face of My Mother*.

Meagan C. Jefferson

An interdisciplinary artist based in North Carolina, Jefferson's creative practice spans poetry and other forms of expression. Her love of literature in adolescence sparked a lifelong passion for writing.

234

Through her work, she explores a range of emotional states, including love, loss, and self-empowerment. Her poetry reflects both personal experience and a desire to connect with others through honesty and resilience. Meagan's poems in this anthology include *Future Love*, *Pocket*, and *Oath of the Silent*.

Mildred M. Stokes

Writing is a massive journey that lifts out of the cocoon of hesitation and doubt, which dim the light of capacity to freely share thoughts. Her poetry book, *I Can Hear You Better with My Glasses On!*, expounds upon actualizations when unhinged conversations flourish. Ahead of that work is *Romancing the Beautiful Divine, A Joy Embrace Story Devotional*, which pulls back the curtains, laced with meditation challenges and prayer blessings which instill reflective spiritual connections. Stokes's dedication to character building continues in her first children's book, *Little Lady Phenola*. In a unique setting of celebration, this story encourages attentiveness, dialogue, discussion and rewards curious readers, family, and friends. Mildred's poems in this anthology include *Ode to Grandma Nissi*, *'E D U M A C A T I O N'*, and *Something Within*.

N.F.G.

A small-town writer, N.F.G. turns to poetry as a way of working through life's challenges. Writing, for him, is both release and re-flection, often emerging in natural patterns that shape his voice on the page. His work has been described as powerful and resonant. He hopes that by sharing his words, readers facing hard times may feel seen and less alone. For N.F.G., poetry is simply about getting the lead out and finding meaning in the process. N.F.G.'s poems in this anthology include *Stuck*, *Engaged*, and *The Rhythm*.

Natalie B. Peterson

An award-winning author and poet of African heritage based in the United Kingdom, Peterson began her writing journey at the age of thirteen. Her work has been recognized in numerous anthologies and competitions, including *Seeds of Inspiration*, *Uplifting Moments*, *In the Mind's Eye*, and *The Healing Word*. In 2013, she published her first book, *The Hands On Inspiration*, and has continued to share her poetry in both forward poetry and United Press collections. Writing has also been a vital outlet in navigating her mental health journey, providing strength and a voice for resilience. Through her work, Peterson hopes to inspire others to embrace creativity and to find hope in life's challenges and triumphs. Natalie's poems in this anthology include *Daffodils*, *B.I.W.I.A*, and *Woman Behind The Smoke (screwballs)*.

Nicole Lanier Montez

An award-winning author and poet, Montez's career spans three decades, during which she has written several poetry books and recorded a spoken word CD. After years in the literary arts business, she realized the need to increase the pool of poetic voices and readers of the written word. In 2015, Montez stepped into the role of poetry workshop facilitator, where she passionately promotes poetry to a bouquet of hues, cross-generations, and a host of genders in Maryland and abroad. Nicole's poems in this anthology include *God Loves Us Too*, *Everlasting*, and *11:59 pm*.

Noah Rivers

An award-winning poet from Barbados, Rivers finds inspiration in the natural beauty of his island, often writing near the water where the rhythm of the waves guides his words. His work explores themes of origin, inheritance, and the bonds that unite humanity across time and space. Through his poetry, he seeks to honor the past while envisioning a more unified future, weaving language that resonates with both personal and collective meaning. Noah's poems in this anthology include *The First Gift: Inheritance* and *No Division in Heaven*.

Q. Denise Masten

An author, entrepreneur, motivator, and serial educator with a deep passion for storytelling, Masten creates works that are visually engaging, interactive, and fun, aiming to inspire readers to embrace a more positive outlook on life. Her goal is for every reader to connect with her stories on a meaningful level and walk away feeling uplifted. Through her writing, she blends creativity and purpose to leave a lasting impact on her audience. Denise's poems in this anthology include *"How Is That Cool?" (Spoken Word Edition)*, *Still Making a Difference*, and *Who Are You? (Spoken Word Edition)*.

Poetic Messiah Willie James Lee III

Lee writes under the name Poetic Messiah, a reflection of his calling to use poetry as both testimony and truth. His work combines rhythm, conviction, and lived experience, offering readers a powerful mix of raw honesty and spiritual insight. Through his voice, he seeks to inspire change, uplift communities, and remind others of the strength found in faith and perseverance. Willie's poems in this anthology include *Poetic Thoughts Pt. 1: The Understanding*, *Just Try Jesus*, and *Rubber Band Man*.

Ren (Robert L. Ellerbe)

Writing since the age of eight, when he won his first poetry contest, Ellerbe discovered a lifelong devotion to words. Known by his pen name Ren, he has gone on to receive several awards for his work, viewing writing not simply as a craft but as his life force. His poetry carries raw honesty, weaving love, loss, betrayal, and survival into verse that resonates deeply with readers. Through his pieces, he illuminates the complexities of relationships and the cost of resilience, offering both confession and catharsis on the page. Ren's poems in this anthology include *Final Goodbye (A Love Letter)*, *Dear Yvette*, and *The Mathematics of Love*.

Ruth Redmond

A mother of three daughters, devoted grandmother, and ten-year breast cancer survivor, Redmond began her career as a certified medical assistant before serving for 27 years with the DC Fire and EMS Department, where she held roles including firefighter-EMT, fire inspector, fire investigator, and hazmat technician. Recently, she embraced her newest role as an author with the release of her memoir, *Within the Fire, I Found My Voice*, and as a poet. Her writing reflects her innovative, creative spirit as a Libran visionary, blending spice, sass, and affirmation in equal measure. Through her words, she shares an authentic and empowering voice that resonates with strength and resilience. Ruth's poems in this anthology include *BLACK ROSE*, *Love Language*, and *I AM*.

Sandra Dawn Swaby Robinson

Originally from Jamaica, Robinson devoted ten years to teaching before moving to America to build her family and provide her son with greater opportunities. She enjoys dancing, cooking, reading, and cherishes time with her loved ones, especially her nephews and niece. Despite the profound loss of her siblings and other close family members, she has remained resilient, leaning on her faith in God. In 2008, she was diagnosed with stage 3 kidney disease, a challenge that deepened her spiritual journey and inspired her to write poetry as a form of prayer and connection. Today, her faith continues to grow, and she trusts in God's grace and mercy to guide her steps forward. Sandra's poems in this anthology include *Homeless*, *Death*, and *Negativity*.

Sean Martin

Born and raised in the Midwest, Martin has been writing poetry since the age of eleven. His work explores the full range of human feelings, from inquiry and reflection to love and redemption. Through his poetry, he seeks to bring joy, spark deeper thinking, and encourage love and empowerment. Writing is both a personal outlet and a catalyst for connecting with others through shared experience. Martin is grateful for the opportunity to share his words and deepest thoughts with a wider audience. Sean's poems in this anthology include *God, I Have a Question*, *On Purpose for Purpose*, and *It's Personal*.

Shantie Morgan

Founder of Evelyn's Closet, a community support hub that provides clothing and essential items to those in need, Morgan created the project as a living tribute to her grandmother Evelyn, whose love, wisdom, and strength shaped her family. A native of Washington,

D.C., she is also a poet and writer whose work draws from her life experiences and personal journey. With a passion for storytelling, she captures both struggle and resilience in her words. Through every change, she continues to hold fast to hope over fear, inspiring others to do the same. Shantie's poems in this anthology include *MK Forever* and *Linwood Edward*.

Sharese Simone

A writer, poet, songwriter, performer, and entrepreneur born in Long Island, New York, and raised in Prince George's County, Maryland, Simone is also a proud mother and advocate for healing work. Known to many as LaLa, she has been writing since childhood and has preserved a rich collection of unpublished works. *Third Quarter Moon* marks her debut publication, offering poems that inspire compassion, self-love, reflection, and empowerment. Through her art, she seeks to cultivate meaningful experiences rooted in vulnerability, authenticity, and intentionality. She continues to embrace creativity as both a personal calling and a way to connect with others. Sharese's poems in this anthology include *My PG County in the 90s* and *His Voice*.

Sh'Quelle Brown

Known as Shaq to her family and Shay to many friends, Brown is a crisis manager in psychiatry who supports people through some of the most difficult days of their lives. She discovered her passion for poetry at a young age, a gift her father nurtured by preserving her earliest grade school work. Brown has since published three collections—*The Garden Beneath My Grief, Between Violence & Valor*, and *Unlearning Forever*—inspired in part by her oldest daughter, Aryianna, who once questioned why she kept her poems hidden in a binder titled *Pages of a Book I'll Never Write*. As a mother of four, she believes in leading by example, showing her children the courage it takes to pursue dreams even when they feel daunting. Through her writing, Brown brings taboo topics, fears, pain, and unspoken emotions into the light, creating space for honesty, healing, and connection. Learn more about her work at www.shquellebrownbooks.com. Sh'Quelle's poems in this anthology include *Breaking Generational Curses*, *Monster In The Closet*, and *QUIET!*.

Sierra Leone Dixon

Writing poetry since childhood, Dixon has long been fascinated by life's many ups and downs and the ways words can capture them. A graduate of Bennett College and longtime educator, she brings the same passion for language to both the classroom and the page. Her work demonstrates a mastery of metaphor, simile, and paradox, creating vivid images that reflect resilience and discovery. Dixon's poetry inspires readers to embrace their experiences fully and to face challenges with courage and hope. Sierra's poems in this anthology include *Thank God for Picking My Mother* and *Dear Daughter*.

T. Smith

Born in Gary, Indiana, and raised in Columbia, Missouri, Smith had the seeds of writing planted at the age of ten. Inspired by the storytelling of her fifth- and sixth-grade teachers, she began writing about issues she felt strongly connected to, drawing from both her imagination and lived experience. She hopes that her work resonates with many readers, offering both connection and reflection. Smith is the author of *Reflections of Me: A Dark Child*, a poetry collection, as well as *Sunny's Days*, a story about her granddaughter's coming of age and the importance of generational family bonds. Through her writing, she continues to explore themes of identity, family, and resilience. T. Smith's poems in this anthology include *Ice Iced Baby*, *Pronouns*, and *Stolen Stories*.

T.A. Broady

Passionate about writing for as long as she can remember, Broady's love for words has evolved into a calling as both an author and motivational speaker. After the passing of her mother, she began writing for an e-magazine and producing motivational videos, channeling her emotions into creative expression. During the COVID-19 pandemic, she rediscovered poetry as a means of reflection, self-evaluation, and healing, addressing both personal growth and the state of society. Her work has since been featured in media productions as a poetic and motivating voice, and she is now a first-time author as well as the founder of Creatively Inspired, LLC. Through her platform, Broady combines her background in journalism, public relations, and human resources with her writing to inspire others to reach new heights with confidence and purpose. T.A.'s poems in this anthology include *What Is Love*, *Without A Doubt, I Say*, and *Black Love Is*.

Tunisia RaWanda

A bold and visionary poet, RaWanda writes with unapologetic honesty about identity, liberation, and the resilience of Black womanhood. Her work—spanning poetry, performance, and her book *Tressed Oūt*—challenges myths while weaving stories, scars, and strands of truth into a mirror her readers can recognize. She creates space for authenticity, healing, and self-acceptance, offering her words as both empowerment and affirmation. Tunisia's poems in this anthology include *Intro: Set My Space*, *B.A.Ū.M*, and *Payne*.

Watson John

Known as Poet Messiah, John hails from Rocky Mount, North Carolina. A U.S. Navy veteran, he seeks to reach the world through the transformative power of poetic expression. Married for 25 years, he and his wife have raised two children who continue to inspire his journey. His work blends imagination, resilience, and faith, offering readers both inspiration and reflection. Watson's poems in this anthology include *Healing*, *Enchanted Forest*, and *The Poet Messiah*.

Acknowledgments

This book is not the work of one, but of many.

It carries the breath of every poet who placed pen to page, trusting us with their truth. To each of you—thank you for your courage, your vision, and your voice.

We are grateful to the editors, designers, and early readers whose eyes and hands helped shape these words into a vessel strong enough to hold so many stories. Your quiet labors gave rhythm and order to this chorus.

To families and friends who stood beside the poets, offering encouragement in late hours and tender moments—we honor you as part of this collective.

And to you, the reader: the circle is not complete without your presence. By opening these pages, you have joined the gathering, adding your listening heart to the sound of the collective pen.

About the Publisher

BookButler Publishing Company (BBPC) was born from a simple belief: words have the power to heal, to challenge, and to transform. We are keepers of voices—emerging and established—who entrust us with their stories, poems, and truths.

Our work extends beyond the printed page. Through literary gatherings, author expos, and workshops, BBPC creates spaces that connect writers with readers and celebrate the transformative power of storytelling. We believe that every pen holds a world, and every voice deserves to be carried forward.

The Sound of the Collective Pen: A Poetry Anthology by Emerging Voices is one such world—woven from resilience, memory, and vision. It is part of our promise to nurture voices that might otherwise go unheard, so that generations to come may know the strength, beauty, and diversity of today's storytellers.

To journey with us further, visit **thebookbutler.com** or follow us across social platforms:

Facebook: @BookButlerPublishing
Instagram: @bbpc.events
YouTube: @thebbpc

www.ingramcontent.com/pod-product-compliance
Lightning Source LLC
Chambersburg PA
CBHW020415150626
46554CB00014B/1440